The Woodhaerst Triangle

Book 1 of The Woodhaerst family drama trilogy

Patricia M Osborne

White Wings

Books

Published 2024 in Great Britain

by White Wings Books

ISBN 978-0-9957107-4-0

British Cataloguing Publication data:
A catalogue record of this book is available from the British Library

This book is also available as an ebook

In Memory of

my dearest mum,

Lila (1932-2014)

and

Sister,

Heather (1956-2009)

Two courageous and inspiring women

A light went out in my heart when you both left this world

Prologue

June, 1953

A high-pitched cry fills the small room as the infant enters the world.

'Is it all right? What did I have?' The girl tries to sit up. Beads of sweat run across her forehead. Her white linen gown is bloodstained.

'No concern of yours, lass. Lie back and let me finish cleaning you up.' The buxom nurse pats the girl down below with a threadbare towel.

It shouldn't be like this. She should've been allowed to have the infant at home, in her own surroundings. Not in this dingy room with an old woman telling her she has no right to know anything. It wasn't fair. 'But the baby's mine. Please, what did I have? Please let me hold it.'

'Take the bairn away'– the nurse waves her large hands at the female attendant – 'take her. Quickly.'

The skinny attendant wraps the baby in white muslin showing only a mass of dark hair.

'A girl. I have a daughter. Please don't take her away. Please. Let me see.' The girl lies back powerless, too tired to even barely move.

Ignoring the young mother, the attendant leaves the room with the infant in her arms. As she opens the door shrieks from another teen in labour echo along the corridor. The heavy door slams shut silencing the screams.

The girl sobs. 'Please.'

'Forget her. She's not yours.' The nurse dips a flannel into a fresh bowl of lukewarm water, wrings it out and washes the sixteen-year-old's face. 'You're a lucky lass. Normal delivery and no stitches. When the time's right, and you have a husband, you can have more bairns. Forget this ever happened. Go home and continue your life.'

Chapter One

Rachel

November, 1971

The bus pulled into Woodhaerst village and stopped at the shelter. My best friend waved from the pavement as I jumped down from the platform. 'Sorry I'm late. Bloody bus. Hope you weren't too cold waiting for me.' I crossed my arms over my chest against the biting wind.

'It's okay, you're here now. 'Fancy Elmo's?'

'Yeah. Good idea. That nice guy works there. Wonder if he'll be in today?'

'You might be in luck.' Linda linked her arm in mine. Why wouldn't Mum and Dad warm to her? They didn't approve of her because she lived on the rough side of town. Not that it made any difference to me. Dad thought very much that I should stick to my own class. Class. What the hell did it matter if you liked a person? She was beautiful. Auburn hair. Huge sparkling green eyes and a smile that could advertise Colgate toothpaste. Being from a working-class area was no excuse for them to be rude about her.

We pushed the glass door open and the wind blew us into the café. It was empty so we had our choice of where to sit.

'Let's go down there.' I made my way to the back and sank into the maroon bench seat. 'Be warmer here, and I can see everything that's going on.' I unbuttoned my coat and enjoyed the blast of warm air. The coffee aroma was strong. I adored the smell of roasted coffee beans.

Linda took the seat opposite me. We'd barely got comfortable when the guy I fancied came across. 'What can I get you?'

'Two coffees, and a teacake to share, please.' I smiled. He was so good-looking. Shoulder length dark brown hair and the most stunning chocolate eyes. I glanced up at the name label pinned on his royal blue top. 'Thanks Joe.'

Once he'd moved away from our table, Linda tapped my wrist. 'He fancies you.'

'Me? Nah.'

'You've gone bright red.'

'Don't.' I put my hands to my face. 'How old do you reckon he is?'

'Seventeen? Eighteen maybe?'

'Hmm. If he's only seventeen that'll make me a cradle-snatcher.'

'That's the least of your worries. Can you imagine what your dad would say?'

'Yeah. Not good enough for me. I'm not sure who he flippin thinks I am. He'd like me to be more like our Jenny. She wants to be a nurse. "You can do better than a dead-end job like Woolworths," he says.'

'If you hadn't come to Woolies then we'd never have met and we wouldn't be going on holiday together next summer.'

'Probably another reason why they don't like you. They'd always hoped I'd go on to Oxford. Said I had the brain. According to Dad you were the one who put ideas into my head about leaving college and working full-time.'

Linda smirked. 'I suppose I did. I liked working with you and wanted you there all the time instead of just on Saturdays.'

We were laughing when Joe came back with our coffees. 'I'm on a break. Would you babes mind if I joined you for a few minutes?' He smoothed his hands down the red-striped apron.

'Go for it.' I said, feeling my cheeks burning up again.

He grinned as he eased himself down on the bench next to me. 'You know my name but I don't know yours.'

'Rachel.' Butterflies fluttered in my stomach. A whiff of his Brut aftershave made its way up my nose making my heart bang.

'And I'm Linda.'

'Hi, Linda,' Joe said before turning back to me. 'Hey, Rachel, how do you fancy going to the flicks with me one night?'

Before I had a chance to answer, Linda butted in. 'Have you got a mate? Only her dad won't let her out on her own.' She beamed.

'Sure. I can ask my pal, Stu.'

'How about Wednesday?' I stirred my coffee. 'We have a half day so can be free earlier.'

'Brill. We'll meet you under the clock tower at six? You won't stand us up though, will you?'

'No, of course not,' I said. 'We'll be there.'

'Cool.' Joe squeezed my hand before getting up. 'See you on Wednesday.' He turned towards the door as a greaser gang bustled in. 'Hi there, guys,' he called before heading over to the noisy crowd.

'How ace is that?' Linda picked up her cup.

'Yeah.' My heart pounded. He was so handsome.

Shivering, I strode over to the brick fireplace and warmed my hands by the glowing embers. I gave them a poke to spring the flames back to life and added a couple of pieces of coal from the scuttle. The bronze-coloured chrysanthemums on the sideboard made me sneeze. Mum liked to have flowers in the lounge all year round but she never considered my hayfever. Grabbing the Lunn Poly brochure, I flopped down onto the cream velour corner sofa and flicked through the pages showing seaside towns but didn't take any of it in. Instead, I was thinking about my date with Joe next week. I couldn't believe my luck when he'd asked me out earlier today.

Jenny wandered into the room, headed straight over to the fire and warmed her hands. 'I hate this weather, and these dark nights. It's only just gone four and look at it.' She padded over to the French doors in her new dusky pink mules and pulled the olive-green velvet drapes together. 'What are you smiling at?'

'Nothing.' I hadn't realised I had been, but my face was obviously showing my excitement about Joe.

'What's that you've got?' She stepped over to the couch and perched herself next to me.

'None of your business.'

'Holiday brochure? Oh aye? When did you get this?'

'In town earlier.'

'Mum was wondering where you'd gone. Did you go to meet her?'

'Shh. Yes.'

Jenny tipped the booklet. 'Planning on going somewhere?' she asked grinning.

'Yes, but shh. Linda and I are going away together next year.'

'Can I come too?'

'No. Go with your own friends.'

'Meanie. You know Dad will never let you go. Not unless I'm with you, that is.'

'Well, it won't be up to him, will it? I'm eighteen so there's nothing he can do about it.'

Mum entered the room wearing the red spotted pinafore apron Jenny had won at a school bazaar. 'Nothing he can do about what?'

'Dinner smells good,' I said, changing the subject. 'What is it? I'm starving.'

'Liver and onion casserole. Your father will be home shortly, so I'd like one of you to set the table.' Mum perched on the arm of the couch and asked softly, 'Now what did I interrupt? Nothing who can do about what?'

'Nothing you or Dad can do about me booking a holiday.'

'Booking a holiday with whom?'

'My friend.'

'You mean Linda Smith? Sorry, Rachel, it's not a good idea. She may be used to going all over the place on her own but you're not.'

'I don't care what you think. I'll be nineteen by the time we go.'

Mum repositioned the amber framed specs on her nose. 'We'll take a family vacation as always.'

'Thanks, but I'd rather go with my friend.'

'You know your father and I object to you hanging around with that girl.'

'I don't know what you and he have got against her. Just because she hasn't got a huge house like us.'

'No, Rachel. It's because we didn't send you to a private school and college to end up in Woolworths as a shop assistant.

That girl's a bad influence. You did well in your exams. You're wasted in that place.'

I took a deep breath. 'Doesn't matter what I do, I'm always in the wrong. You should be happy that I'm happy. I love it at Woolworths so I don't care what you and Dad think. And I couldn't care less whether you like my friend or not.'

Mum stood up away from the sofa. 'Your behaviour since you finished college is disgraceful. You've become disrespectful and far too argumentative.'

'Well, you'll be able to have a couple of weeks rest from me when I'm on my hols. Won't you?'

Mum shook her head and tutted. 'Your father will have something to say about this, young lady. You mark my words.'

'Have you found somewhere to go?' Jenny asked.

I opened up the brochure. 'We're thinking here, Blackpool' – I flipped the pages – 'or here, at New Brighton. I can't wait.'

Jenny tossed her long blonde hair away from her face. 'It does look nice, Mum' – Jenny passed her the booklet – 'take a peep.'

Mum brushed it away.

I snatched the brochure back from my sister and slammed it down on the glass coffee table. 'I don't care what any of you think. I'm going away with my best friend and there's nothing any of you can do about it.'

Chapter Two

Peggy

I stirred the tea in the pot and poured a cup for myself, Adam and Kate. My sister, Sheila, had bought us the set for Christmas last year. I wondered what she'd get us this time. The teapot was an unusual shape, more like a coffee pot, but I liked it, particularly the green abstract pattern. Maybe I'd suggest matching dinner plates. That is if she hadn't already bought our gift as the festivities were less than seven weeks away. It was hard to believe that in two months we'd be entering nineteen-seventy-two. Where had this year gone?

Kate added milk to a small bowl of cornflakes then shovelled them into her mouth far too quickly.

'Slow down, our Kate,' Adam said resting *The Echo* on the Formica table. 'You'll give yourself stomach ache. What's the rush?'

'I'm late. I've still got my PE kit to pack. You should've woken me earlier, Mam.'

'Now, now, our Kate. Don't go blaming your mam. Tell you what' – Adam tapped the back of her hand – 'why don't I drop you off? I can go into work a little later.'

'Are you sure, Dad?'

'Anything for my girl. The first MOT isn't booked in until eleven so it won't cause a problem.'

'Thanks, Dad. You're the best.' Kate leaned over and pecked her father's cheek.

I scooped bacon and eggs from the frying pan onto the plate and placed it in front of Adam. 'Here you go, darling. Just the way you like it.'

'Thanks, love.' He playfully patted my bottom as I swung past him.

'Urgh. Do you mind?' Kate got up from the chair, shaking her head as she left the kitchen. 'They're at it again,' she joked to her elder brother, Neil, as they crossed paths in the doorway.

'What's she on about?' He yawned.

'Nothing. You should come home earlier, son.' Adam took a slice of toast from the rack and dipped it into his egg.

'Don't start, Dad.'

'Would you like a cooked brekkie or cereal, Neil?' I asked.

'Neither. I've just come in to grab my keys.'

'At least have a bit of toast. You can't go to work on fresh air.'

'If it keeps you happy.' Neil grabbed the last slice in the rack and left the room chewing a chunk of toast.

Adam brought over his dirty dish to the sink where I was washing up. 'I'd best get going too if I'm going to get our Kate to school on time.' He planted a huge kiss on my lips. 'See you later, love.' He made his way into the hallway and I followed.

'You ready, Kate?' he called upstairs.

'Coming.' She scrambled down lugging her satchel.

I opened the front door ready for them to leave. 'Have a good day, both of you.'

'And you, love.' Adam blew me a kiss before climbing into the driving seat.

I pulled the small wooden box from the back of my wardrobe and took out an old photograph. I'd been thinking about Mike a lot lately. Things could've been so different. I slumped onto the bed, closed my eyes, and let the memories flood in.

Mike had swaggered into the dance hall with another bloke, both dressed in steel blue uniforms. Tawny hair fell across his forehead. Butterflies consumed me. Edna at the factory had convinced me to go on a blind date with her and her boyfriend. 'That's them. Mine's the one with the blond hair.' She nudged me. 'What do you think of yours?'

'Very dapper.'

Edna waved to the boys to attract their attention. They caught her eye and swaggered over. The blond-haired one kissed Edna on the lips. 'How's my gal?'

'Good, thanks. This is Peggy.'

He turned to me. 'Hi, Peggy, I'm Pete and this is my chum, Mike. Mike's your date for this evening.'

'Hi, Peg,' Mike said, 'you don't mind if I call you that, do you?' He didn't wait for an answer before taking my hand. 'Let's dance.'

'All right.' I let him lead me into a jive. My legs trembled as this handsome guy twirled me around.

I opened my eyes and chased the memory away. *Stop it, Peg.* I was so naïve in those days. I was about to get up and pop the photograph back when I drifted off in thought again about another dance after Mike and I had been dating for a while.

We were coming out of the village hall, Mike with his arm around me. 'Let's go over there and have some quiet time.'

He led me to the adjacent field, placed his jacket down on the ground and patted his coat. 'Come on, Peg.'

Nervously I lowered myself onto his jacket and allowed him to smother my neck with kisses. He stopped for a moment and gazed into my eyes. 'I know we've only known each other for a few weeks, but I'm falling in love with you. Do you feel the same?'

'Yes,' I whispered.

He cupped my breast, making me tingle. After a minute or so he ran his fingers up my leg. I pushed his hand away. He continued kissing, and groaning, but it wasn't long before his hand was back. I pushed it away again. He explored under my blouse and around my back. Expertly he unfastened my bra before I could stop him.

'I want to marry you, Peg,' he muttered caressing me. 'You're so beautiful.'

Before I knew what was happening his hand was up my skirt. Oh my god. I should've stopped him but I was mesmerised and madly in love.

Afterwards he held me in his arms. 'I wish we could stay here all night,' he said, 'but I need to get back to the barracks. Don't worry though, I'll walk you home first. Are you okay? You know, from...?'

I nodded. I was sore but ecstatic. Mike loved me and I loved him.

Stop it, Peg. I got up off the bed and shoved the photograph back in the box. That was the past. I was betraying Adam with these thoughts. Adam was the kindest husband a woman could wish for and a wonderful father. And it wasn't really Mike I was yearning for but my baby girl. I carefully tipped the keepsakes from the box, and cradled the tiny pair of white booties I'd knitted when first discovering I was expecting. She'd be eighteen now. I wondered whether she was happy. Things should've been so different. Pulling myself together, I returned the booties to the memory box, and re-hid it at the back of my wardrobe.

I should get a job. That's what I should do. Now that the kids were older there wasn't enough to occupy me at home. I went downstairs, picked up the local newspaper from the sideboard, and scanned the Classified Ads.

The doorbell chimed.

'Are you expecting anyone,' Adam asked.

I looked at my watch. Nine o'clock. Who'd be coming here at this time of night? I shook my head. 'No.' I went to get up from the settee but Adam gently pressed my upper arm.

'You stay there. I'll get it.'

'Sheila. Come in,' I heard him say before showing my sister into the sitting room. She'd been crying, and was soaked from the rain.

I jumped up and hurried over to her. 'Whatever's the matter? And what are you doing out at this hour?'

'He's gone, Peggy.'

'Who?'

'Dad. I've just come from the hospital.'

Why should I care? He stole my right to bring up my firstborn. As far as I was concerned he died over eighteen years ago.

Sheila sobbed on my shoulder. I put my arms around her. 'Adam, get a towel will you, love?'

'Sure.' He left the room.

'I know there was no love between the two of you but surely you must feel something?' She sniffled.

I wanted to tell her I did, but I couldn't. That would be a lie. Instead, I patted her on the back and said, 'There now. I'm here for you. You must stay the night.'

'Thanks, Peg. I'd appreciate that. Malc's on the nightshift and I don't want to be alone.'

'Let's get this off you.' I slid the wet gaberdine away from her shoulders as Adam came back in.

'Here you go, love.' He passed me the towel and took Sheila's wet coat. 'I'll hang this over the bath.'

I turned the knob up on the gas fire. 'It'll warm up soon.'

Sheila kicked her shoes off and curled up on the sofa.

'So, what was it?' I asked, rubbing her hair dry. 'What finished him off?'

'A massive heart attack. As you know he's had a couple since Mam died and this one was just too much for him.'

'I'm sorry.'

'Are you really, Peg?' She turned her head to look at me. 'Does that mean you'll come to the funeral?'

I blinked. 'You'll have Malc. I don't want to be a hypocrite, Sheila.'

'But you came to Mam's.'

'That was different.'

'He often asked about you and wondered why you didn't come to the house.'

'Because I couldn't bear to look at him. And he knew that. Look Sheila, I don't want to fall out with you because I know you loved him and you're hurting but I can't forgive him for what he did. It was unforgiveable.'

'But what did he do?'

'I don't want to talk about it.'

Adam came back in with two mugs of hot tea. He placed them on the teak coffee table. 'Get that down you, Sheila. It'll warm you up. I'm sorry to hear about your dad. The bed in the spare room's made up ready.' He patted her arm. 'I'll leave you girls to it.'

Against my better judgement I went to the funeral with Sheila. When Dad's coffin was carried back down the aisle, she gripped my hand tightly, almost drawing blood.

We followed the pall-bearers out to the graveyard. They came to a halt at the ready dug hole. It was already bitterly cold without the weather deciding to send huge hailstones to slap our faces. I didn't listen as the vicar gave our father his rites to committal. Why was I even here? I knew the answer. I couldn't let my younger sister face this alone. She loved our dad but then she'd enjoyed a better relationship with him than me. It was almost like we'd had different fathers. Perhaps he'd given up the demon drink after I left home. Would he have done what he had if he'd been sober?

Sheila squeezed my hand. 'Thanks for being here, Peg.' She sniffled, wiping her nose. 'I couldn't do this without you,' she whispered.

She had Malc, why did she need me? Adam had offered to come and support me but I wasn't having any of that. There was no need for him to lose a day's pay when I was standing at a stranger's grave. I wasn't here to mourn but to support my sister. The kids had never met their grandparents. We told them my parents had disapproved of their dad and they'd accepted that. Adam and I were now the only ones alive who knew what my father had done.

Finally, the coffin was lowered into the ground. Sheila buried her head into my chest and sobbed. Malc stood by redundant, stroking her back.

'Come on,' I said, once it was over, and led her away from the graveside. 'Let's get you into the warmth.'

Malc took the car keys from his pocket. 'I'll run on ahead and get the car started.'

'Thanks, Malc.' I guided my sister along the shingle path.

⸻

Back at my sister's flat I didn't recognise any of the mourners. Malc was a good host and took over things while I consoled Sheila. She'd finally calmed down as we chatted over tea.

'The landlord's only given me a couple of weeks to clear out the house. Will you help me, Peg?' She nibbled on a ham and tomato sandwich.

'Yes of course.' There was no way I'd leave her to do that alone. 'We'll get someone in to do a house clearance for the furniture and you and I can go through the paperwork.' I wasn't particularly happy with the idea of going through Mam's stuff ten years after she'd passed but Dad hadn't let her things be touched. Despite being a drunk and a rotten father to me, he seemed to have loved Mam, and our Sheila. But then Sheila hadn't shamed the family. I seethed just thinking about it.

I set my cup down on the coffee table. 'Look, I need to go. I should get home to make tea before the kids and Adam get in.'

Sheila sighed. 'Oh. I was hoping you'd stay to the end.'

I had to get out of there. If one more person offered me their condolences, I think I may have screamed. 'You can manage this now. I don't even know these people. If you'd like me to come over later to help clear up then I will.'

'No.' She squeezed my fingers. 'No. We'll manage.'

'I'll see you tomorrow then at ten o'clock?'

The house was freezing. It felt eerie stepping over the threshold after all these years. Thank goodness I'd had the sense to ask Sheila for a key. She never was the best timekeeper. It was now twenty past ten. I found a box of Swan Vestas on the hearth, struck a match, and the gas fire burst into life. It should warm up soon in this small room.

I was back here nineteen years ago when Dad found out I was having a baby.

He'd slapped me across my face. 'You dirty little slut.'

I touched my face now. Still remembering the sting. And then his next words. 'You can get rid of it.'

'No,' I screamed. 'Mam, don't make me.' I'd heard of girls going to these places and getting butchered and not being able to have any more children. Anyway, Mike was coming back for me. We'd get married and he'd take me away from this hole.

'It's too late for an abortion,' Mam said.

'Well, she's not keeping it. She can go to a mother and baby home before she starts to show. Leave it to me. I'll sort everything. I won't have her shaming us.'

My father had been a hypocrite who shamed us all with his drinking.

The sound of a car engine drew me to the window. I lifted the nets. Finally, Sheila had arrived. She got out of the maroon Ford Anglia, and her husband drove off. I opened the front door. 'Morning or should I say afternoon?'

'Sorry, Peg. We got stuck in traffic. I'll put the kettle on and we can get warmed up. Have you been here long?'

'I got here at the time we agreed. The fire's lit so warming up nicely. I boiled the kettle but forgot to bring milk. Did you bring any?'

'Yep' – she patted her shopping bag – 'in here.'

I followed her into the kitchen and reheated the kettle on the gas ring. She dug into the bag and waved an old medicine bottle with milk in it, and a packet of Rich Tea at me.

'Great.' I stirred the pot before pouring the tea into the mugs. 'Where shall we start?' I placed a few biscuits on to a plate.

'The bureau, I suppose. We should find the life insurance policy.'

We took a shoebox of paperwork each and set to work. Me on the armchair and Sheila on the two-seater couch. The same suite that had been here all my life. An awful gold-mustard that didn't look like it had been cleaned since Mam died.

'I think this is what you're looking for.' I passed her an Eagle Star policy.

'Thanks.' She unfolded the document. 'Wow. Five thousand. That'll help.'

'I don't want any of it.'

'We're both named as beneficiaries. Whatever you thought about Dad, he still loved you.'

'Well, he had a funny way of showing it.' If he'd loved me then he wouldn't have done what he did. Yes, he loved our Sheila but I don't think he'd ever shown me an ounce of affection. Even before I shamed him, as he put it. I wondered what had happened to change him? Maybe he hated me, and once I was out of the picture, he became a decent human being.

'Hang on,' Sheila said, 'this is addressed to you but it's been opened.'

I held my hand out. 'Let me see.'

She passed me an airmail envelope, not taking her eyes off me. 'Read it.'

I stared at the December 1952 date stamp and unfolded the sheet to reveal only part of the page with an American address in the top right-hand corner and *My darling Peg,* then nothing. The rest of the letter had been ripped off. I'd no idea what had been written but it must've been from Mike as I didn't know anyone else in America who'd be calling me darling. There was no way of knowing whether he was breaking up with me or coming back to marry me as he'd promised. Who had done this? It had to have been Dad. And why had he kept the address? Had he replied to Mike?

'What is it, Peg? You've gone as white as a sheet and why are you crying?'

I passed the piece of paper.

Sheila scanned the note. 'But it doesn't say anything.'

'Exactly. The letter's been read and destroyed. He kept it from me. Why would he do that?'

'I don't know. Who was it from? Could you write as there's an address?'

'I'm not sure Adam would appreciate that. Anyway, it's rather nineteen years too late. Mike's probably not at that address anymore and he could be married too.'

'Mike?'

'Forget it.'

'Is Mike why you hated Dad so much?'

'Partly. But I've told you before I don't want to talk about it. You loved him and it wouldn't be right, especially now, if I turned you against him. I just feel so sad to think I thought he wasn't interested in me. My life could've been so different.'

'But then you wouldn't have met Adam and had Neil and Kate.'

'That is true but Dad had no right to do this to me.'

Chapter Three

Rachel

Linda met me off the bus and we hurried over to the clock tower. The village was quiet as not a lot happened in the evening.

'We should have no trouble spotting the lads,' Linda said.

'Hopefully not, because it's flippin' freezing.' I tightened the brown cashmere scarf around my neck.

'There's Joe now' – she pointed – 'and that must be Stu. He looks a bit of all right.'

The boys crossed the road and strode towards us. 'Hello babe,' Joe said. He kissed my cheek before turning to my friend and saying, 'Linda, this is Stu.'

Stu smiled. 'Hiya, Linda.'

Linda's eyes sparkled.

'Fancy a coffee?' Joe scratched his head. 'The film doesn't start until just after seven.'

'Elmo's?' Stu asked.

'Nah. Not there,' Joe said. 'How about up the road at Oasis?'

I turned to Linda. She shrugged. 'Okay,' I said.

Joe held my hand as we strolled up the cobbled lane. 'James Bond all right for you babes?' he asked. 'It's the latest one, *Diamonds are Forever*.'

Linda and I nodded. I'd heard good things about it but I didn't suppose we'd watch much of the film anyway. I was excited at the thought of sitting in the back row with Joe.

The bell dinged as we pushed open the door into the spacious café. Joe paced his way to the back and we all followed.

'I'll get these,' he said.

'Are you sure?' I asked, aware that he and Stu were still at college so only worked part-time.

'Yeah, I'm sure.' He beamed. 'Four coffees it is then.' Joe went up to the counter while the rest of us took a seat.

'So, you both work at Woolies then?' Stu asked.

'Yep.' I slipped off my coat and placed it on the back of the chair. 'I've only been full-time since September but Linda's been there for nearly four years. She's a supervisor. I've got the best deal though because I'm on the sweet counter with those lovely Brazil nuts.'

'Pear drops are my favourites.' Stu laughed. 'You'll have to bring me a quarter next time.'

So, there was to be a next time. I felt the Cheshire cat grin growing on my face.

⚜

Joe and Stu insisted on paying the picture entrance for me and Linda. We made our way to the back row. The thought of sitting so close to Joe for the next couple of hours made my pulse go mad.

He slid his arm around me and I snuggled into his shoulder smelling his gorgeous *Brut* aftershave. Gosh he was handsome with his long hair, leather jacket and tight green T-shirt accentuating his slim physique. I tried to keep my eyes on the screen but couldn't concentrate as my heart was doing double-unders. Joe rested his fingers on my knee. I gazed up at him and he kissed me. During the film, every now and then, we'd sit up for a glimpse to see what was happening and then go back to snogging.

Stu nudged Joe. 'Hey, Davies, you're missing the best bit.'

We sat upright. Bond was having a fight with someone in an elevator. I winced as the guy went over the railing and fell to his death.

'It's okay,' Joe whispered, 'it's not real.' He turned to snog me again and before we knew it the credits were up on the screen.

'Can I see you again?' Joe asked me as we left by the exit.

'Sure. When?'

'How about Sunday? We could go for a walk, or if it's too cold, the pub?'

'Linda and Stu too?'

'If that's what you'd like.'

'I would.' I checked the time on my watch. 'I need to catch the bus.'

'I'll give you a lift if you like. I've got my bike.'

'A bike?'

'Yeah. I have a motorbike.'

'Cool. What make?'

'BSA. It's only a 250cc but once I'm eighteen I plan to get a bigger one. Do you know about bikes?'

'Not really but I've always fancied having a ride on one.'

'Come on then. Stu, I'm giving Rachel a lift. Make sure Linda gets home safely.'

'Of course. You know me, always the gentleman. Good to meet you, Rachel. See you tomorrow, Davies.'

Linda's eyes lit up. 'Ta-ra then, Rach.'

'See you tomorrow.' I grinned.

Joe guided me across the road to his motorcycle. It was a gorgeous shade of sapphire blue. He helped me up on to the pillion. 'Where am I going?'

'Arundel Avenue. The other side of town. Do you know it?'

'Sure. The posh part.' He brushed my arm, resting his fingers for a few seconds. 'Just lean with the bike. Give me a tap when you need me to stop.'

'All right.' I fastened my scarf across my ears and under my chin to keep warm.

Joe started the engine, pressing his foot on the throttle, and pulled away. Wow, this was exciting. Dad would have something to say about this. The roads were quiet and in no time at all my street was in view. I tapped Joe on his back, and shouted, 'Over there will do.'

He parked the bike against the kerb and climbed off before helping me down. He took me into his arms like earlier at the pictures and we snogged some more until coming up for air.

'I'd better go otherwise my dad will be out looking for me. See you Sunday.'

'I can't wait.' He got back on the bike, revved the engine, and disappeared with speed.

I sauntered up the avenue to my house. Even though it was bitterly cold outside, I was warm as toast. I couldn't wait until Sunday. I was in love. Joe and I had hit it off like we'd known each other forever. I pushed open the front gate, ambled up the garden path, and turned the key in the lock.

Chapter Four

Rachel

I stomped across the room to the settee where Dad was reading *The Sunday Times*. 'You know you can't stop me going on holiday with my friend?'

He dropped the open newspaper onto his lap. 'While you're under my roof young lady, I can do what I like.'

'Then I'll move out.'

'Don't be so stupid.'

'I'm not. Linda's mam said I can stay at theirs.'

Dad shot up from his seat. 'What's got into you?' He rubbed his nose. 'As if I didn't know. It's that slut you're always hanging around with.'

'Don't call my friend a slut. She's not, and I'm nineteen in a few months, that's what's got into me. You can't keep treating me like a child and telling me what I can and can't do.'

He lifted his hand as though to strike me.

'Going to hit me now? Wait until Mum hears about this. I'm going to get ready.' I stormed out of the lounge, upstairs and into my room. Who did he think he was? I was an adult not a kid. I banged the wardrobe door open and pulled out my white polo neck jumper and lilac tartan skirt. I smiled, flopping down on the bed. I'd wear these today. Linda had said I looked a million dollars when I tried them on in the boutique. Joe wouldn't know what hit him. I slipped out of my jeans and T-shirt and stepped into my new stuff. The skirt was four inches above my knees showing off my slender, shapely legs. No doubt Daddy Dear would have something to say about it. I looked in the mirror, swaying. My long, dark hair gleamed red tints under the light. I dug into my make-up bag and patted green powder on my lids bringing out the brown in my eyes and brushed the mascara wand across my lashes coating them black. To finish off I traced a plum lipstick around my lips. I smiled at my reflection, gave myself a nod of approval, picked up my handbag and crept downstairs. If I could sneak out before Mum or Dad saw me then that would be one less row.

'Just one moment, young lady.'

I turned to see Mum standing with her hands on her hips.

'Where do you think you're going without a coat?'

'Oh. I forgot.' I made my way to the hallway cupboard and unhooked my faux suede Afghan and laid it over my arm as I headed to the back door.

'Not so fast.' Dad's voice came from the sitting room. 'Come and say goodbye before you take off.'

I took a deep breath and headed into the lounge. I really didn't want to have another argument.

He peered over his newspaper. 'I think somebody's forgotten to put their skirt on.'

'What?' I raised my voice. 'How dare you? This is new.'

'You're not going out like that. Get back upstairs and change. And while you're there, wipe that muck off your face.'

'No. I won't. And I'm not changing either. I love my outfit.'

'You have far too much leg showing. Has your mother seen what you're wearing?'

'Yes, and she doesn't mind.'

'I don't believe that for one moment. You'll get yourself into trouble wearing clothes like that and your face made up like a tart.'

'How dare you? I don't look like a tart. And all the girls my age are wearing this length. It's the fashion. And they all wear make-up.'

His face went redder. 'I said go and take it off.'

I stamped my feet. 'No.'

'Get changed now. You look like a little tramp.'

Jenny was at the door entrance. She rushed away calling, 'Mum, come quickly.' She hurried back with Mum in tow.

Mum wiped her hands on her apron. 'What's all the shouting?'

'Nothing, Rosalind, a misunderstanding, that's all.'

'It's not a misunderstanding, Mum. He called me a tramp.'

'Charles?'

He shook his head. 'That's not what I said. She refused to change her clothes and I said she looked like a tramp. And she does. Just look at the length of her dress.'

Mum squinted. 'It is a little short, Rachel. Why not do as Dad asked and wear something else?'

'Because I don't want to. It's not that short. Everyone's wearing clothes like this. You're both just old-fashioned. I'm old enough to decide for myself what I should wear.' I darted out of the room, slipped my arms into my coat and slammed the front door but not before I heard Dad say, 'She'll end up just like her.' What did he mean by that? I wasn't going back to find out though.

Linda met me off the bus and we headed to the clock tower where the lads were waiting. From a distance they looked almost identical. Both in leather jackets, long hair, similar height and build. We waved and they waved back and made their way towards us.

'Hiya, babe.' Joe bent his head towards me, tickling my face with his hair as he kissed me on the lips. 'I've missed you.'

'I've missed you too.'

'Fancy a drink?' he asked. 'There's a nice little pub, The Half Moon, about half a mile away. We can cut through Maple Park.'

'Sounds good to me.' I glanced at Linda. 'What do you reckon, Lind?'

'Fine with me. I like it there. I think it's quite quaint.' She took hold of Stu's hand as we wandered across the road and down a dry-mudded footpath into the park which looked a little sad with the maples bare. Only a couple of months ago they'd been a picture of red and gold. At least the sun was shining so it didn't feel too cold and my new Afghan helped.

Joe pushed the pub door open. We were greeted with laughter and chatter from the saloon bar. As I followed him into the small lounge I had a coughing fit from the haze of smoke.

'You okay?' Joe asked.

'Yep, I'll be all right once I get a drink.'

He took my hand and led me to an empty booth at the back with panelled walls and red lampshades. Quaint, Linda had said. Not quite the word I'd use. Pokey more like.

'Sit yourselves down,' Joe said, 'while Stu and I'll get the drinks. What would you like?'

Linda clasped her hands and fiddled with her thumbs. 'Half a Woodpecker please. You want the same, Rachel?'

'Yeah, thanks,' I managed to say after the coughing finally stopped. 'I'll get the next round.' I slipped off my coat and laid it across a spare stool.

The lads went up to the bar and ordered from the bald-headed bartender. He peered across at Linda and me. 'Are they old enough?' he asked loud enough for us to hear.

'Yep. They're eighteen,' Joe answered.

'If you say so.' The bartender pulled back the lever on the pumps and drew two pints of bitter and placed a jug of cider and half-pint glasses on the counter.

'Cheers.' Joe handed him the cash.

Stu strode over with our drinks and put them on the table. 'I'll just go back and help Joe.'

'Thanks.' Linda filled our glasses with cider from the jug.

I sipped the alcohol and pulled a face.

'You'll get used to it.' Linda chuckled. 'I can't believe you've never had a proper drink.'

The boys returned with their pints. Joe dug into his pocket and threw a packet of nuts onto the table. 'We can share.' He took a slurp of his beer. 'The bartender thinks you two are underage.'

'That's a joke' – Linda gave a horselaugh – 'when we're legal and you two aren't.'

Stu offered his packet of Woodbines. I'd never smoked before but thought, why not? Everyone else did. He flicked the lighter and I drew on the cigarette. The first couple of drags made me cough. I'd show Dad who was an adult or not.

We wandered out of the pub and went next door to the Off License and bought a couple of big bottles of cider to drink in the park. I made a point of paying. The boys carried the booze and we made our way to a bench in a shelter to protect us from the wind. We passed the bottles around in turn, each taking a swig. What with the alcohol and smoking, I was feeling a little giddy.

'Don't worry,' Joe said, 'I'll see you home on the bus.' They hadn't come on their motorbikes as they knew they'd be drinking.

I snuggled up to Joe to keep warm and we snogged a bit until Stu interrupted us and said, 'Linda tells me you're going on holiday together next year?'

'Yep. Blackpool or New Brighton. Why?'

Stu winked at Linda. 'Joe and I have been chatting about going to Spain next year to celebrate our eighteenths. You should go there.'

'Spain. That's not a bad idea. What do you think, Rach? Fancy going on a plane?'

'Yeah, why not?' That would irritate Dad a little more.

'We can pick up more brochures at lunchtime tomorrow. But we'll need a passport.'

'Don't we need photos for that?'

'Yep, but we can get them from the kiosk in work. You'll need your birth certificate too.'

'Oh. I'll have to find that.' I couldn't believe that I'd never seen my birth certificate but then I supposed there'd never been a reason to. 'So where should we go in Spain?' I asked Stu but Joe answered.

'Benidorm is where all the fun happens. And maybe if...'

'What?' I asked.

'I was going to say if we booked the same time, and we're all still together, you and Lind could come with us –' he shook his head – 'but that was a daft idea. Far too soon.'

'We can talk about it later,' I said. Joe obviously felt the same way as me. We may have only just got together but it was love at first sight. I checked my watch. The time had moved on and it was getting dark. 'We should go.' I stood up and smoothed my coat down. 'The last bus today is at half past six and if you're coming with me and then have to get back, we should hurry.'

With only five minutes to spare, Joe took my hand and we ran across to the bus stop, arriving just as it pulled up. After boarding we climbed up the narrow staircase and made for the back seats. No one else was up there so I cuddled up to Joe and he started kissing me, brushing his hand against my breast. We didn't even hear the conductor until he coughed to let us know he was there.

'Less of that on my bus if you don't mind. You youngsters.' He tutted. 'Where to?'

'Top of Arundel Avenue please.' I handed twenty pence in coins. He reeled out two tickets which I stuffed into my pocket. 'You should stay on when we get there,' I said to Joe, 'as it goes back to town, and it's the last one.'

'Okay. We'd best make the most of our time now then.' He slid his hands into my coat and we had a quick snog.

Reluctantly I pulled away. 'That's my stop coming up.' I rushed downstairs with Joe behind me. He gave me a quick peck on the cheek before I jumped off. I waved at him as he got comfy on the bench seat.

Chapter Five

Rachel

Mum had promised to sort out my passport form but after a week had gone by I was still waiting. I knew it was a ruse to stop me going on holiday with Linda. My parents had gone out so I took the opportunity to go into Dad's office which was out of bounds when he wasn't around. After listening in the hallway, to make sure Jenny wasn't about, I turned the knob and crept in, quietly closing the door behind me. It had to be in his desk. I rummaged through the drawers but I couldn't find it. Only bills and other forms I didn't understand. I tried the top drawer but it was locked. Dad dropped something into the pen pot the other day. I emptied it out and picked up a small key, popped it in the lock and it turned. Yes, this was the right place. I grinned. Mum and Dad's passports, their marriage certificate. I pulled out the bundle of papers. What was this? Adoption. My head spinning, I sank into Dad's swivel chair. Adopted. No, surely not, but...

I rushed to the bathroom to be sick. Oh my God, who was I? Had I read it wrong and it wasn't me at all? I needed to check. I washed my face and hands before returning. The certificate stared back at me. There was no mistake. It clearly stated I was adopted with Mum and Dad's names. What was the reason for this? Was my mother unmarried? If so, she still could've kept me. Linda's mam was unmarried and she'd kept her. Why didn't my mother want me? And why hadn't Mum and Dad told me?

I sank back into the chair. It all made sense now. The reason they were all blue-eyed and fair while I was dark-haired with brown eyes. And those comments Dad had been making lately. *She'll end up like her.* What should I do now? Should I try to meet her? Would I be able to find her? Would she even want to meet me? I squeezed my eyes shut to stop the tears but it didn't help. Once I started crying, I couldn't stop. I didn't know who I was anymore. And that was Mum and Dad's fault. They should've told me. I shouldn't have had to find out like this. I was eighteen years old, there'd been plenty of time to tell me. With the certificate in my hands, I sobbed, wishing it not to be true.

The front door banged closed and heavy footsteps came down the hallway. Dad shouted, 'What the hell are you doing in here? You know this room is off limits.'

I dropped the documentation to the floor. 'I wanted my birth certificate but I found...' I felt like I was going to faint.

'What's going on?' Mum was at the door with Jenny.

'I found Rachel snooping around in my office. The girls know this room is private. This is the last straw. You can tell she's...'

I took a deep breath and managed to get the words out. 'She's what, Dad?'

'Nothing' – he shook his head – 'just get out of here and we'll forget all about this incident.'

'The thing is, Dad, I can't forget.' I picked up the certificate and held it out. 'It says here I'm adopted? I can't believe you didn't tell me.'

Mum rushed to my side and put her arm around me. 'We'd always planned to, darling, but there never seemed to be a right time. We didn't want this.'

'What do you mean, this?'

'You all upset. It didn't matter to us that I hadn't given birth to you. You're still every bit our child.'

'And what about her?' I pointed to Jenny. 'Is she adopted too?'

'No. No, Jennifer isn't. After trying for over five years we thought we couldn't have a baby. Then after we got you, well it was like magic. The doctor reckoned it was because we'd both relaxed. Within three months I was expecting.'

'I still don't know why you didn't tell me. Now everything makes sense. Why you all look alike and the old joke I suffered from friends at school that I must've been the milkman's. And the snidey comments Dad's been making lately. You should've told me.'

Mum kneeled beside me. 'Your dad and I didn't want you to think that we loved you any less than Jennifer. Just because you were adopted.'

'Mum. Help,' Jenny shouted. 'It's Dad.'

Mum looked up. 'Charles? Charles, are you okay?'

I turned to him. His face was red as he gripped his chest. 'What's happening?' I asked.

Mum ignored me, picked up the phone handpiece, and dialled. 'Ambulance please. I think my husband's having a heart attack.'

⋆

Mum had gone to collect Dad from hospital. They'd kept him in for a few days and concluded it was angina. 'Not usually life threatening,' they'd said, 'but more a warning.'

I wanted to know more about my adoption but didn't want Dad to have another funny turn. It seemed I'd have to be patient. Jenny and Mum had constantly been reassuring me that the adoption made no difference, but it did to me. I felt incomplete, like I'd lost my identity.

Tyres crunched on gravel and I peered out of the window to see Mum pulling the car into the drive. I made my way to the kitchen and put the kettle on, popping three Tetley teabags into the pot. When I wandered into the hallway they were already inside and Mum was speaking quietly to Dad. 'Remember, darling, rest, and no getting stressed.'

'I'm sorry, Dad.' I kissed him on the cheek. 'How are you feeling? I've got the kettle on for tea.'

'I'll be fine, love.' He patted my arm. 'It wasn't your fault. Give me a bit of time and I'll answer all of your questions. I'm sorry we didn't tell you. We did what we thought was best.' He moved over to the couch, lowered himself down on it, and put his feet up.

'It's all right, Dad. I know.' I propped two scatter cushions behind his back. 'Like Mum said, you must rest, I can wait.'

'Thanks, honey. I do feel rather tired.' He closed his eyes and within seconds he was snoring.

Mum grinned. 'Let's go and have that cup of tea.'

Chapter Six

Rachel

The lounge looked bare without the Christmas decorations. Nothing had been mentioned about my adoption since Dad had that angina attack back in November and I was too nervous to ask in case he ended up in hospital again.

Although everything was the same as usual during the festivities, I felt like an intruder, like I no longer belonged. At least I'd get to see Joe tomorrow. I hadn't mentioned being adopted to him or to Linda because I didn't want them looking at me as if I were a different person.

After sucking up pine needles from the carpet with the vacuum cleaner, I slumped onto the sofa. I wasn't sure why I had to clear up when the cleaner was due tomorrow. Mum said it couldn't wait. Jenny had escaped the chores by going out with her friend and I was left like Cinders out of Cinderella. Dad had asked me to stay at home but hadn't said why. Obviously to do the cleaning.

My parents wandered in. Dad sank into the armchair opposite while Mum took the seat beside me on the couch.

'Have I done something wrong?' I asked.

'No. Not at all.' Dad rubbed his blond moustache. 'We're ready to answer your questions now.'

I sat upright. 'Is that why you didn't want me to go out?' I felt guilty for assuming I was being treated like the less perfect daughter.

'It was.' Dad fiddled with the medium sized brown envelope in his lap. He coughed. 'Where shall I start?'

'What do you know about my mother?'

He pulled a sheet of paper from the envelope and studied it. 'She was only sixteen when she gave birth to you.'

'That was young.' I couldn't even imagine having a baby now, and I was nineteen in six months. 'Do you have a name?'

'Yes, we do. Margaret Carter. Although it says here, also known as Peggy. We've an address too. It was on the back of a photograph, so we're assuming it was hers. No one mentioned it at the time and we just put the photo away until now. Before I give you the address, we'd like you to be very sure that it is what you want. You may open a can of worms. We don't know anything about her parents other than your maternal grandmother was a housewife and your grandfather a labourer.'

'There's nothing wrong with manual labour, Dad. People don't have to be executives or directors to be good people.' My stomach flipped. 'Does it mention my father?'

'No details other than he was an American in the forces and nowhere on the scene when you were born.' Dad took out a small photograph from the envelope and passed it to me the reverse side up.

'East Cross. Isn't that the small village just the other side of Woodhaerst?' I asked.

'Yes,' Dad answered. 'It's just a couple of miles from Chester.'

She lived that close? Maybe she still lived there? I wondered if I'd served her in the shop. My pulse vibrated. I turned over to the black and white picture. 'Is this her?'

'Yes,' Dad answered, 'and we believe the younger girl is her sister.'

Peggy looked nice. Long wavy hair. A fifties floral swing dress showing off her small waist. I wondered what colour it was. Perhaps white with red roses. 'She's pretty,' I said.

Mum and Dad nodded.

'Her sister doesn't look very old. About six?'

'We don't know that detail. What we do know is that your mother was deemed intelligent at school.'

I laughed. 'So that's where I get my brains from.'

'Very possibly.' Mum's eyes filled.

'Oh don't, Mum. This doesn't make any difference to how I feel about you and Dad. You'll always be my parents, but you understand why I need to know?'

Dad answered, 'Yes, we do, but...'

'What?'

'Please.' Mum squeezed my hand. 'Please, think it over before rushing in.'

'I will.' I smiled, my heart drumming as I stared down at the picture of my mother. I was going to find out who I was. 'Thank you. Thank you for this.'

≈

'Jenny.' I pulled her in from the front door entrance.

'What is it? It's not Dad again, is it?'

'No. Nothing like that. I've got some news. Get your shoes and coat off and come to my room.'

'Can I at least get a hot drink?' She passed me her coat. 'Hang this up,' she said, pulling off her platform shoes.

'Sorry. Of course. I'm just so excited. Let's put the kettle on.' I dragged her into the kitchen. 'Sit down and I'll make you a cuppa. Or would you prefer hot chocolate?'

'Chocolate please.'

After pouring milk into a small saucepan and placing it on the electric ring, I stretched up to the cupboard and reached for the tub of Cadbury's.

'So, tell me then? What's your news?' Jenny sank into the wicker dining chair, crossing her legs.

'Mum and Dad, well Dad really, told me about my mother.'

'Did you nag him? You know he has to avoid stress.'

'No, I never said anything. It all came from him.' I tipped the almost boiling milk into two mugs.

'Where are Mum and Dad now?'

'They've gone for a walk. Dad said he needed some exercise.' I swirled three heaped teaspoons of chocolate powder into each cup and stirred. 'There you go.' I handed her a mug. 'Let's go up to my room in case they come back in.'

Jenny followed me upstairs to my bedroom, put her mug down on the bedside table, and curled up on my multicoloured patchwork quilt. 'Go on then.'

'Well' – I climbed on the bed next to her – 'I've got an address.'

'For your mother?'

'Yes.'

'What are you going to do?'

'I'd like to try and find her but suppose she doesn't want to see me?'

'I don't understand why you'd want to see her. She's a stranger. Your real parents are Mum and Dad. But if that's what you want...'

'Well obviously I don't want to upset Mum and Dad but I do want to know my roots. You know?' I passed her the picture. 'Do you think I look like her?'

'I see a likeness around the eyes.'

'Do you think so?'

'I just said so, didn't I?'

'Her name's Peggy. She was only sixteen when she had me.'

'God. Imagine having a baby at that age. No wonder she gave you up.'

'Linda's mam was only seventeen.'

'Maybe she had support.' Jenny studied the photograph. 'Who's the girl next to her?'

'Her sister, apparently. My aunt. Although Dad didn't have any details about her or how old she was. She looks about six, don't you think?'

'Something like that. That would have been a big age gap. I wonder if there are any siblings in-between.' She handed the photo back to me. 'Now, let's get back to the problem in hand. Are you going to try and meet her?'

'I think so.' I glared at the address on the back of the photo. 'If I go, will you come with me?'

'If you like. But you know she may not live there anymore?'

'Yes. I realise that. I've a half day Wednesday so we could go then. You could meet me outside Woolies at one o'clock as you have no college that day. We'd tell Mum we're going shopping.'

'All right but I don't like lying to Mum.'

<hr/>

I pressed the bell to request the bus to stop. Jenny and I stepped down to the pavement at the bottom of Sedgwick Avenue. Terraced houses were lined up either side of the road, each with a small walled garden.

'We want number sixty-one.' I squinted at the numbers near me. 'This one is a hundred and twenty-four. We need to cross over and move up the road. And leave the talking to me.'

As we approached number sixty-one, a house with a green door and low hedge above the wall, a woman came out. Was that her? She looked young.

'Hello,' I said, 'we're looking for Margaret Carter. Peggy.'

'Peggy? That's my sister, what do you want with her?'

'My mother's very ill and is asking to see her.'

'Oh, I see. Sorry to hear about your mother. Strange our Peg's never mentioned a friend who's ill.'

'Mum's been living in America for the last nineteen years, so they kind of lost touch, but they were close friends before that. And since returning home she keeps asking for Peggy.'

'Look, jot down your details and I'll pass them on to my sister. She hasn't lived here for years.'

'Thanks. I took a pen from my handbag and wrote down my name, address and telephone number.'

'I'll be in touch then, Rachel.'

'Thanks.'

The woman got into a maroon car and the man at the wheel started up the engine.

Butterflies fluttered in my stomach. 'She must be my aunt.' I smiled, shoving the piece of paper and pen into my coat pocket. Today I was one step closer to finding my real mother.

Chapter Seven

Peggy

Sheila got up from the couch and put on her coat. 'Oh, I nearly forgot. When I locked up Dad's house for the final time two teenage girls stopped me. The elder one, Rachel, I think was her name, said she was looking for you.'

'She asked for me?'

'Yeah.'

'Hmm, Rachel. I'm not sure I know a Rachel.' My heart beat faster.

'She said her mother had returned from America very ill, and had asked her to find you. It seems you were close friends nineteen years ago. Obviously, I didn't give out your address.'

America. Was Mike back? He wanted to see me. What would Adam say about that? No, it couldn't be Mike, otherwise why would a teenager come looking? 'Thanks. Did she leave a contact address?'

'Yeah, and a phone number.'

'I can't remember any friend going to America. Maybe it was someone from school. Let me have the number and I'll contact her to find out more.'

'It's at home. I'll tell you what, shall I ring her, and pass on your address?'

'No. I'd rather not give a stranger my details until I know what's what. Ring me when you get in, but don't forget. If the woman's sick I may be too late.'

'I'm really sorry, Peg. I should've remembered.'

'It's all right.' I tapped her shoulder. 'You've had a lot going on.' I tried to sound casual but inside I was beginning to hope this Rachel was my daughter.

'I won't.' She looked at her watch. 'Malc will be wondering where I've got to. I'd best go.' She pecked me on the cheek. 'Ta-ra then, Peg.'

'Bye, Sheila.' I closed the door behind her. My heart was racing. It had to be my daughter. Who else could it be? There was no way Mike would come looking for me after all these years. My prayers were being answered.

⁂

Adam held my hand as we meandered along the road. I loved how he still did that. I'd suggested an early evening walk so we could chat without Kate listening in. Neil was out again. He was hardly in these days. Perhaps he had a girlfriend.

The weather was mild for February. As we approached the local park the sea of yellow crocuses made me smile.

'What's this about, Peg? Something on your mind?'

'You know me too well.'

'What is it?'

'You know Sheila was here earlier?'

'Yes. She's okay, isn't she? I thought she was doing better.'

'She is, but just before leaving she said something strange. She mentioned a teenage girl had been around Dad's house looking for me. The thing is, Adam...' My heart pounded. I sensed an involuntary grin creeping across my face, 'I think she might be my daughter.'

'Your daughter? Hey, slow down. Don't go jumping to conclusions. Why do you think she might be your daughter?'

'She said her mother was very ill, and wanted to see me, that we'd been old friends before she moved to America.'

'Hmm that does sound like she could've been sending you a message.'

'Yes' – I squeezed his hand – 'that's what I thought. I can't believe this is happening. I know we've spoken about this day but are you all right if we meet her?'

'Of course. I've always said that. Did you say anything to your sister?'

'No. Not yet. Not until I know. And of course, then we'll need to tell the kids too. How do you think they'll react to the news?'

'They'll be fine.' Adam kissed my cheek. 'Don't worry, love. This sounds like good news.'

'Thanks, darling. What would I do without you?'

He pulled me closer. 'You'll never have to find out.'

'I tell you what. Why don't we pop into The Rising Sun while we're out and I'll treat you to a pint?'

'A smashing idea. Come on, I don't need asking twice.' He laughed.

Chapter Eight

Peggy

Adam came in from the hallway carrying the post. 'This one's for you, love.'

I checked the postmark. It was from her. Six weeks ago, Sheila had rung through Rachel's details, but I was too nervous to speak on the phone so I wrote to her instead. Since then we'd been corresponding and in my last letter I'd asked her if she was ready to meet.

'Are you going to open it or just study it?' Adam stroked my cheek.

'I suppose I should.' My hands trembled as I ripped open the envelope, and scanned the words on the page. 'She's agreed to meet and suggested next Wednesday at the clock tower in Woodhaerst. What should I say?'

'Say, yes, of course.'

'Suppose she doesn't like me.' I dabbed my damp eyes.

'Hey, come here.' Adam took me into a hug. 'How could she not like you? She'll fall in love with you.'

I brushed my lips against his. 'Thanks, love. I'll write back saying I'll be there.'

He released me from his hold. 'Isn't she on the phone? And didn't Sheila give you the number?'

'Yes, she did.'

'Wouldn't it be easier to ring?'

'I suppose so.' The letter shook in my hand. 'But I don't think I'm strong enough to make the call.'

'Why don't I phone?'

'You'd do that?'

'Of course I will. It'll save time rather than hanging around for the post both ways. You're a nervous wreck. If you have to wait around too long, I dread to think of the state you'll be in. I'll do it now.' Leaving the door open, Adam made his way to the telephone in the hall, picked up the handpiece and dialled the number. 'It's ringing,' he said. 'Hang on, someone's answered.' He spoke into the mouthpiece. 'May I speak to Rachel Webster, please.' He covered the mouthpiece. 'She's just getting her.' Adam cleared his throat. 'Hello there, Rachel. This is Adam Davies. I understand you've been corresponding with my wife, Peggy.' He nodded. 'Yes, that's right. Quarter past one. Yep, she'll be there. She's looking forward to meeting you. Bye for now.' He put the phone down and returned to the room.

My hands were shaking. 'But suppose she doesn't like me.'

'I've already told you, she will.' He wrapped his arms around me to try and stop my trembling. 'She's bringing her sister. Would you like me to come with you?'

'Would you? But what about work?'

'I'll book a day's holiday. If she has her sister then you need some moral support too.'

'What did I do to deserve such a wonderful husband like you?'

Chapter Nine

Rachel

I returned the phone receiver to its cradle and wandered back into the lounge.

Jenny lowered an opened book to her lap. 'Who was it?'

'It was Peggy's husband. You remember we met her sister?'

'She's finally got in touch then?'

'Er, not exactly. To be honest, she got in touch with me weeks ago but I didn't feel like telling anyone and we've been writing to each other since. In her last letter she asked if I was ready to meet.'

'Meet you where? What's going on? I don't understand.'

I sank into the sofa next to Jenny and handed her the crumpled envelope from my pocket. 'This was her first letter.'

Jenny pulled out the note and read aloud.

> *Dear Rachel,*
>
> *My sister says you were enquiring after me, that your mother, a friend of mine is ill. I am deducing that this is not so, and that you've found out about your origins. I've thought a lot about you over the years and would love to meet whenever you feel ready.*
>
> *Yours truly,*
>
> *Peggy Davies (nee Margaret Carter)*

'But she doesn't exactly say she's your mother?'

'She does in the the next letter.'

'Can I see it?'

'Sorry, that's private, as are the others, and I'd rather not show them to you.'

'Okay. Fair enough.'

'In her last letter she asked if I was ready to meet, and I wrote back saying I was, and suggested next Wednesday. I'm really nervous though so will you come with me?'

'28, Broadbridge Drive. Isn't that over West Heaton way?'

'Yes, I think so. But I suggested we meet at the clock tower, and that was her husband confirming she'll be there. So will you come with me?'

'If that's what you want.'

'It is.'

Jenny shrugged her shoulders. 'Wouldn't you rather take Linda?'

'No. I don't want anyone else knowing I'm adopted yet. I know it's daft but it's made me feel less of a person.'

'That is daft. But yes, I'll come with you. Can I get back to my book now?' She stuck her head into *The Exorcist*.

'I'm surprised you don't have nightmares reading that.'

She laughed. 'Who said I don't?' She put the book down again. 'What about Mum and Dad? Are you going to tell them?'

'Not yet. And as they're out and don't know about the phone call there's no need to answer any awkward questions.'

'You know how I feel about lying to Mum and Dad.'

'Me too, but it's just for this visit. I'll tell them afterwards once Dad's had his check-up.'

'I suppose that's wise. But you owe me.' She jabbed my arm.

'Yep, I do. Thanks, sis.' I headed out of the lounge and upstairs to my bedroom. My stomach churned with excitement.

I was finally going to meet my mother. My adoptive parents would always be Mum and Dad but this compulsion to know where I'd come from wouldn't go away. I rummaged through my wardrobe wondering what to wear next week to make a good impression.

Grabbing my latest purchase, a leather jacket, I rushed out of the front door and down the road.

Joe was leaning against his motorbike. 'Hi babe, you've brought the sunshine. Love the jacket. Climb on.'

I put my foot up on to the platform, my leg across the pillion, and backed up in position, leaving room for Joe at the front. I was used to motorcycle riding now as we'd been going out together for six months. No one knew about us though besides Linda as Mum and Dad would have put an end to it. It didn't matter that I was almost nineteen.

Joe spun his head round. 'Ready?'

I gave him a thumbs up and he revved the engine and sped down the road. It was wonderful having the wind blowing through my hair. After zooming past cars and through two sets of traffic lights, we rode into the entrance of Maple Park where we'd arranged to meet Linda and Stu. We were greeted by a bed of daffodils waving their yellow and orange heads. Joe parked the bike and we wandered over to the pavilion hand in hand. I so wanted to tell him about next week's meeting with my mother but at the same time I didn't want him to think less of me. Instead, once we were comfortable on a bench, I fell into his arms. We were so engrossed that we didn't hear Linda and Stu turn up.

'Don't you two ever stop?' Stu asked. 'I'm surprised you don't get a room in a motel.'

'We're not ready for that yet.' Joe laughed.

I giggled, but silently I didn't want us to get a room at all as I wasn't ready to lose my virginity. Linda and Stu had moved on to the next stage but it wasn't for me. Mum had brought me up that it was something you did on your wedding night and that's what I wanted. So far Joe hadn't put any pressure on me.

'What are we going to do?' I asked.

'Let's stay here for a while.' Stu pulled Linda down on to the bench and began snogging her.

'Is that okay with you, Rachel?' Joe snuggled back up to me.

'Yeah sure.' I returned my lips to his.

Our ecstasy was broken when out of nowhere a female voice yelled, 'You should be ashamed of yourselves.'

I peered up at a woman with a Yorkshire Terrier on a lead and a toddler in a pushchair.

'Sorry.' I moved away from Joe.

'So you should be. This is a public park you know, and I don't want my child seeing you leather jacket yobs getting up to no good.'

'We were only kissing,' I said.

'Up to no good. I've a good mind to report you for carrying on like that on a Sunday afternoon in a public place.'

Stu leapt to his feet. 'Buzz off you old bat. Weren't you ever young? Or is it you're not getting it anymore now you've got a lad?'

The kid in the pushchair started screaming. His face turned red.

'Stop it, Stu. You're upsetting the boy.' Suppose this woman reported us. Worse still suppose she came into Woolies and recognised me or Linda. I hid my face. 'Look, Mrs, we're really sorry. We'll go now.' I zipped up my jacket.

Linda prodded me. 'What did you say that for?'

'Because she may recognise us if she comes into the shop,' I whispered, getting up and stretching my hand out for Joe to take. 'Let's go.'

The black and tan dog started yapping and pulling while the toddler was still screaming. 'All right, Toby.' The woman turned to us with one last scowl before racing down the path with Toby in the pushchair and the yelping terrier.

Joe drew me back to the bench.

'No' – I pulled away – 'I want to go.'

'Okay, babe. We'll go and get a coffee.'

We headed over to the pavilion café and chose a table by the window. Linda and I went up to the counter and ordered drinks.

'Two strawberry milkshakes, a black coffee and a tea, please?' I handed over fifty pence.

'I'll bring them over,' the red-haired lad said after passing me my change.

'That was such a giggle.' Stu roared with laughter and Linda joined in with her horselaugh.

'It really wasn't funny.' I brushed loose strands of hair from my ponytail behind my ears.

'Here's our drinks. That was quick.' Joe leaned back into his seat to allow the waiter to put our order down.

Stu slurped his strawberry milkshake and burped loudly. Linda chuckled. Goodness knows what my parents would make of their behaviour and if they ever found out that I'd been snogging on a park bench they'd disown me for sure.

'It was a hoot,' Stu continued.

'I don't want to talk about it anymore.' I blew into my cup before taking a sip of my coffee.

Linda slapped my hand. 'Don't be such a prude.'

I felt my eyes sting.

'Leave her be,' Joe said. He put his arm around me.

'Do you mind taking me home, Joe? I'm not feeling that great.' I put my cup down.

'Of course, babe. I'll just finish my tea. You're okay though?'

'I'm feeling a bit sick and I've got work tomorrow so think I should rest.'

'Sure.' He tipped the mug to his mouth, emptying its contents, and placed it down on the table along with a five pence tip. 'You two coming?'

'Nope. We're going to hang around here for a while. I'll see you at college tomorrow.' Stu put his arm around Linda and planted a kiss on her lips.

As we hurried out of the café I said, 'I'm really sorry to have spoiled your day.'

'That's all right. I can see you're upset. Come on, let's get you home. I've got some studying to do this evening anyway. Me mam'll be pleased to have me home early for once.'

Chapter Ten

Peggy

Adam wrapped his arm around my shoulder while we waited under the clock tower. Crowds dashed along the pavement as customers and staff left the shops for half day closing.

I glanced at my wristwatch. 'She's late.'

'Only a few minutes. Give her a chance. She could be delayed.' He squeezed me closer. 'Don't worry, she'll be here. She contacted you, remember.'

'Yes, but I'm the one who pushed to meet.'

'Wait look' – Adam signalled with his head – 'across the road. There she is.'

I squinted. 'How do you know?'

'Because she's the image of you. How your Sheila didn't pick up on that, I don't know.' Adam waved to the two girls. They increased their pace to an almost run and slowed as they got closer. Rachel appeared as nervous as me. The other girl took her arm and pulled her along. They stopped on reaching us.

'Margaret Carter?' the fair-haired girl asked.

'Yes, that's me. But call me Peggy, please.' I looked to the other young woman. 'Rachel?'

'Hello.' She lowered her head.

'Let's go over to Oasis and get some hot drinks to warm us up,' Adam suggested. 'It's a bit chilly for April.'

The girls nodded. Adam took my arm and led me along the path. We reached the café and he took the lead in selecting a table at the back. I slid in first and the girls sat opposite.

'Right. What would you like?' Adam asked, sitting down next to me.

Rachel looked tense. 'Hot chocolate please,' she answered before turning to her sister, 'Jenny?'

'The same, please.' Jenny frowned, looking like she'd rather be somewhere else.

'And something to eat?' Adam scanned the menu. 'Cake, pastry or something else?'

'No thanks,' Jenny said.

'Me neither.' Rachel smiled, relaxing a little.

'Just a black coffee for me please, love,' I said, unable to contemplate eating anything with a million butterflies fluttering in my abdomen.

'Right you are. I'll go up and order.' After patting my leg he got up, made his way to the short queue, and stood behind two other people. He turned and winked at me.

'So, Peggy, I hope you've got some answers.' Jenny folded her arms.

'I'm happy to answer all of Rachel's questions.'

Rachel kept her head down studying her steepled hands. Why didn't she want to look at me? My heart raced. This wasn't quite how I'd imagined the first meeting with my daughter. I breathed with relief when Adam returned with two cups in his hand. 'Hot chocolate for the girls. I'll just go back and get ours.' He put his arm around my shoulder. 'Everything okay?'

I nodded, feeling anything other than okay.

'I'll be back in a sec.' He squeezed my hand.

Jenny stirred her hot chocolate. 'So, why did you give my sister up?' She was certainly pushy. I wished Rachel hadn't brought her.

I coughed. 'Er...'

I was saved by Adam as he placed our coffees down and slid back next to me. 'Have you come in on the bus?'

'No, I came straight from work, but Jen was on the bus so I had to wait for her.' Rachel took a sip from her cup.

Jenny bolted upright. 'Enough of the small talk. We're not here to make new best friends. It's information we want.'

Rachel nudged Jenny. 'Don't.'

Adam scowled at Jenny. 'Are you always so rude, young lady? I won't have you pushing my wife about like that. I think it would be a good idea if you and I picked up our drinks and moved to another table and let Peggy and Rachel get acquainted without any interference.'

Jenny glared at Rachel. 'I'm not going anywhere.'

Rachel nudged her sister. 'It's okay, Jen. I think I'd like to speak to Peggy on my own. If you don't mind?'

Jenny shrugged her shoulders. 'Suit yourself but I'll wait outside.' She got up and made for the door leaving her hot chocolate on the table.

Adam pressed my fingers. 'I'll just be over there if you need me.'

'Thanks love.'

'It's wonderful to finally meet you. I've waited so long for this day to arrive.' I stretched my arm across the table and took Rachel's hand.

She pulled away, and said in almost a whisper, 'Why did you give me up?'

I bit my lip. 'I didn't... Like I said in my letters, it wasn't my choice.'

'I know you said that but I still don't understand. My friend's mam wasn't married and she managed to keep her baby. So how come you didn't?'

'It wasn't a one-night stand or anything like that, if that's what you're thinking.' I took a deep breath. 'You were made from love. I remember you growing inside me.' I put my hand across my stomach. 'I was so excited to hold you in my arms but...'

'What?' Rachel blinked.

'They took you away before I got a chance to even see you. All I saw was your head of dark hair.' I squeezed my eyes to stop any tears escaping.

'Is he my father?' She signalled across to Adam.

'No. No. He's not. I met Adam just after you were born. I told him all about you on our first date and we always hoped this day would come. I'd almost given up after not hearing anything and then out of the blue you turned up at my late father's house.'

'I only found out I was adopted back in November when I was looking for my birth certificate. Instead of a birth certificate, I found a document about the adoption, and then Dad had an angina attack ending up in hospital, and he was only up to talking about things after Christmas.'

'I see. That must have been a shock.' I stirred my coffee.

'It was. Apparently, my parents thought they couldn't have children which is why they adopted me and then like a miracle Mum ended up being pregnant with Jenny just afterwards. I always wondered why I had brown eyes and dark hair when they were all fair and blue-eyed.'

'Well, I'm really pleased you decided to find me.'

'What about Adam though? Does he feel the same?' Rachel took a sip of her drink.

'Like I said, we both always hoped you'd come looking.' I turned to the window and spotted Jenny glaring at me.

Rachel caught her too. 'I'm so sorry. Excuse me, I'll be back in a moment.' She stormed out of the café and grabbed her sister.

If only I was able to lip-read as I couldn't hear what they were saying.

Adam came over. 'Is everything all right?'

'Yes, at least I think so. Rachel's gone to sort her sister out. Mind you they'll get drenched as it's started raining. You couldn't tempt her back into the dry, could you?'

'Sure. Leave her to me.' Adam strode out of the door and over to the girls. He said something to Rachel. She smiled and made her way back in and sat down.

'I'm sorry about that. Jen can be a bit overprotective.' Rachel's brown eyes twinkled. 'Adam's trying to coax her back indoors. He's quite a charmer. I almost wish he was my father.' She grinned. 'Oh look, it seems he was successful.'

Adam returned with a soaked Jenny, despite the brolly in her hand, and led her to his table.

'Now, where were we?' Rachel took a sip from her hot chocolate.

'I was telling you how pleased I was when you made contact, and although at the time I wasn't one hundred per cent you were my daughter, like I said in the letter, it was your cryptic clue that gave me hope.'

Rachel laughed. 'Yes, a bit of quick thinking from me. I didn't think it would be appropriate to introduce myself as your daughter.'

'No. Thank you for that.'

She licked her lips. 'You do know that us meeting won't change things with my parents. They'll always be my mum and dad.'

'Of course. I wouldn't expect otherwise. After all they're the ones who've brought you up.'

'But you can be my Peggy. Mum and Dad have been so supportive. It was Dad who gave me your address' – she passed me a photograph – 'it was on the back of this.'

'Oh yes I remember this being taken.' I'd no idea Dad had passed these details on. Perhaps he wasn't all bad after all. Or maybe it was Mam.

'What about my father?' Rachel took the photo back and dropped it into her handbag. 'Can I meet him?'

'I've not seen Mike since before you were born. He was over here from the States, stationed at Sealand Air Base, which is why I was thrown a little when you mentioned America in your message. For a moment I thought it might have been him trying to contact me but that would be absurd after all this time. We were to be married. He was supposed to send passage for me but I never heard from him after he left to be restationed in Texas. It was awful, I thought he might be dead. There had to be a reason why he didn't send for me. We loved each other. We really did.'

'That must have been hard for you. With you being so young?'

The waitress came along. 'Two toasted teacakes.'

Rachel and I glanced at each other. 'We didn't order any,' I said.

'The gentleman over there did.'

I glimpsed across at Adam. He smiled and held up his thumb.

'Thank you,' I mouthed, but knew there was no way I'd be able to stomach a crumb.

The butter melted as Rachel spread it on the hot bun. 'They do look tasty.' She took a bite. 'So how come they made you give me up?'

I cleared my throat. 'Dad was furious when I was expecting. Mam was all for me keeping the baby. Even happy to say the child was hers, like lots of mams did then, but he wasn't having any of that. He booked me into a mother and baby home before I started to show and once you were born, I never even got a chance to hold you. I begged them.' I took my hanky from my pocket and wiped my eyes. 'They wouldn't let me. They

56

wouldn't even tell me whether I'd had a boy or girl. It was only when the nurse let *she* slip that I knew I'd given birth to a daughter.'

'Why wouldn't they let you hold me?'

'They said you were to be adopted and there was no going back.'

Chapter Eleven

Rachel

'It's flippin freezing.' I folded my arms across my chest. 'We're supposed to be in the middle of April not December. I wish the bloody bus would hurry up.'

Jenny slapped my hand. 'Don't let Mum hear you speaking like that.'

'Why didn't you like Peggy?'

'I just don't trust her. Anyway, you know you mean the world to Mum and Dad? We couldn't have better parents. Look. Here's the bus.' Jenny stretched out an arm to signal the green double-decker to pull over.

We stepped up onto the platform. The bus started moving before we got to the top of the narrow stairway. 'Hold on tight,' I said. No one else was up there so we made our way to the front seats. 'I thought she was nice.'

'Are you going to meet up with her again?'

'Of course. Why? Don't you think I should?'

'No. I don't.' She frowned. 'And I don't believe she couldn't have kept you. If she'd really wanted you, she should've fought for you.'

'It's a good job she's not your mother then, isn't it? Anyway, I want to find out more about my father.'

Jenny glowered. 'It's up to you, but Mum and Dad aren't going to like it.'

'Maybe once I know my father's full name and what regiment he was in, I can trace him too. Wouldn't it be exciting if he still lives in America and I have the chance to visit?'

'If you say so.'

'Maybe I should get Linda to go with me if you're going to be snidey.'

'Tickets.' The bus conductor rattled his tray.

I opened my purse. 'Two to Arundel Avenue.'

'That'll be twenty pence.'

'Thanks.' I offered up the coins.

He wound the machine handle and handed me two tickets which I popped into my pocket.

'You and that Lind...' Jenny muttered under her breath.

'Leave it out, Jen. Come on. Ours is the next stop.' I got up from the seat and rang the bell, making my way downstairs, with Jenny behind me. We held on to the rail at the bottom and skipped off the bus once it had stopped.

Jenny put up her umbrella. 'Do you want to come under?'

'No, you're okay. It's only spitting.'

'Suit yourself. Are you going to tell Mum and Dad?'

'Yes, providing Dad's check-up went well. I don't want to lie to them, even if they do drive me mad sometimes. They'll understand I want to know my roots.'

Jenny stuck her nose up in the air. 'Sure they will. You don't know how lucky you are. You could've ended up with a poor family like Linda Smith. Instead, you've never had to want for anything.'

'That's easy for you to say when they're your real parents.'

We trekked home the rest of the way in silence. Thankfully the rain hadn't come to much. I wondered what my father looked like. Peggy certainly had good taste in men if Adam was anything to go by. He was such a gentleman.

'I'm famished.' I picked up the dish of pilchards in tomato sauce and served a portion onto my plate. 'Can you pass the salad please, Dad?'

His light blue eyes sparkled. He was quite good-looking when he smiled but he hadn't had a lot to smile about lately. What with the heart business and me asking questions about my adoption. He'd always been a good dad, well that was until I left college and went to work at Woolies on a permanent basis. Since then, he hadn't stopped moaning at me, complaining about the length of my skirts, my choice of job, and my friends. But I had to try harder to be pleasant because I didn't want him to end up with a full-blown heart attack.

'How did the check-up go,' I asked.

'Good. They don't want to see me again for another year. My blood pressure's down and the ECG was normal.'

'That's really good news.' I picked up a cherry tomato and stuck it into my mouth whole.

'Rachel.' Mum frowned.

'Sorry, Mum, but have you ever tried cutting into them? They burst all over the place.'

Mum shook her head. 'What have you girls been up to today?'

I glanced at Jenny. She glared back at me. I turned to Mum and said, 'Actually, we met my mother today.'

Dad put his cutlery down. 'You did what? I'm surprised you didn't speak to your mum and me about it first?'

'Sorry. I should've done, but I didn't want to mention it until after you'd been to the hospital.' I poured water into my tumbler from the smoked glass jug.

Mum sighed. 'Oh Rachel, no good can come from this.'

'I did as you asked, Mum, and gave it a lot of thought. She was nice. Really nice.' I put a forkful of pilchard and lettuce into my mouth.

'Are you going to see her again?' Mum helped herself to a chunk of French bread from the basket in the centre of the table.

'That's my intention. We didn't set a date but I'll phone her later to arrange another meet up, when I hope to find out more about my father.'

Dad picked up his cutlery and moved the food around his plate. 'You're rushing into this. Just like you always do. You never stop to think things through.'

'That's not true. I did as you both asked and took time to think about it. We've been writing to each other for weeks. You just don't want me to get to know her.' I scowled at Jenny who had a huge grin on her face as if to say *I told you so*.

'Your mum's right,' Dad said. 'This isn't going to end well.'

'You don't know that. Just because that's what you're both hoping for.'

Jenny took a sip from her glass. 'I didn't like her.' She licked her lips. 'I think she was lying and Rachel's better off without her. She doesn't need her. She has us.'

'Perhaps you should listen to your sister,' Mum said. 'Jennifer has always had a wise head on her young shoulders.'

'Why can't you be more supportive?' My stomach churned. I hadn't expected such a battle on my hands. 'I don't care what any of you say, I'm phoning her after dinner.'

Mum and Dad glanced at each other shaking their heads. Mum tutted. 'It will end in tears. Just you wait and see.'

Chapter Twelve

Rachel

I grabbed my handbag off the banister. 'Mum, I'm going now. I shan't be long.'

'Be back for your tea,' she called out.

I couldn't believe it was over a week since I'd met up with Peggy. This time there'd just be the two of us. I was on my way out the front door when Jenny grabbed me. 'Are you going to meet her?'

'What if I am?'

'Because I told you, I don't trust her.'

I pushed her hand off my coat. 'Mind your own. This has nothing to do with you.'

'It'll end in tears just like Mum said.'

'Oh shut-up.'

Jenny shrugged. 'Don't come crying to me.'

I slammed the door behind me and ran to the bus stop.

⋘

Peggy waved from inside the Wimpy Bar. I rushed in. 'Sorry I'm late.'

'You're not. I hope you don't mind but I took the liberty of ordering for us both.'

A waiter, who looked about sixteen, came to the table. 'Two knickerbocker glories?'

'Yes, that's us,' Peggy said.

The lad set a tall cone-shaped glass down in front of each of us before moving on to a table across the other side of the café.

'I hope you like these.' Peggy pointed to the desserts.

'Not half. They're my favourite. Thanks.' I dug the long spoon into the ice cream.

'How have you been?'

'All right.' I put my spoon down. 'In fact, really good,' I lied. 'I told Mum and Dad about you and they've been really supportive.'

'That's wonderful. I'd hate to think meeting up with me would cause waves in your relationship?'

'No worries there, well except for my snidey sister.'

'Hmm, I got the impression she didn't think much of me. Perhaps she's worried that you won't want your family if you have a new one?'

'Well, she has no concern there.' I frowned. 'I'll always want my family.'

'Sorry, I didn't mean anything by it. Of course, you will.'

I spooned up the jelly and fruit from the bottom of the glass. 'Changing the subject, how did you know I'd like this?'

'Well I didn't but hoped you would as my kids love a knickerbocker glory.'

'Neil and Kate? You mentioned them in your letters.'

'Yes, that's right. Neil's not that much younger than you. He's eighteen in October and Kate's sixteen in July. We'll be having a joint garden party for them in August. You should come.'

I turned away.

'What is it, Rachel? Have I said something to upset you?'

'No. No, of course not.' I stirred the empty dessert glass, avoiding eye contact.

'There is something? We were getting on so well and now...'

I dropped the spoon to the table. 'I'm sorry but if you must know it's...'

'What?'

My chest pounded. 'They've had you for all their birthdays while you never gave me a single thought on mine.' I made eye contact. 'There. I've said it. Now you can see what a jealous cow I am and you're probably glad that you had me adopted.'

She reached across and took my hand. 'I don't think that. It's understandable you'd feel like that. You were always on my mind though. And...'

'What?'

'Every year I bought a birthday card for you. I'll bring them next time and you can read them. And keep them. They're yours after all. I named you too. You were my Christine.'

'Christine?' I smiled. 'I like it. You can call me that if you like?' I felt like I'd become two people. Rachel the daughter of Mum and Dad, and Christine the daughter of Peggy. 'What about my father? Will you tell me more about him?'

'Yes, of course. Shall we get a coffee first?'

'Would you mind if we went for a walk? We could go for a wander around the park. The spring flowers are out. I love Nature. Don't you?'

'Yes, I do. I'll just pay for these and then we can go.'

I ran my fingers over her black patent leather bag. 'This is lovely.'

'It is rather, isn't it? Adam bought it for me last Christmas. Why don't I buy you one?'

'That's very kind but...'

'I owe you eighteen birthday presents. Let me, please? Perhaps we could meet one day in the week and go to the shops so you can choose.'

'I'm not sure.'

Peggy raised her hand to get the waiter's attention as he cleared the table behind. 'Can we have the bill please?'

'Sure.' He finished wiping down the table, went over to the counter, tapped on a calculator, and wrote on his notepad, returning with the bill. 'Here you are.'

'Thank you.' Peggy took some coins from her snakeskin purse and handed them over. 'Keep the change.' She returned the purse to her handbag and snapped it shut. 'Shall we go?'

⸎

It was boiling so I slipped off my Afghan coat. 'This weather's so changeable. Last week it was freezing and now it's in the seventies.'

'Let's hope that means we're going to get a good summer.'

We sauntered past magnolia trees blooming star shaped white flowers, and the cherry blossom which was in full bloom. As we reached the pond, Peggy asked, 'Shall we sit on that bench for a while? I'm not used to so much walking.'

'Sure.' We'd been touring the park for over an hour and I was learning a lot about her. 'Oh look, goslings.' Eight bundles of caramel and cream fluff hid under their Egyptian mother's wings.

'They're so cute,' Peggy said, lowering herself to the metal seat.

Once we were both settled, I brought up the subject of my father again. 'You still haven't told me about my father. I know you have a sister, that you didn't get on with your dad, you like knitting, have two other teenagers, but you haven't told me about Mike.'

'I'm sorry. Let me tell you about him. He was very handsome.'

'Did he have dark hair like me?'

'Not quite. You get that from me. His was more a tawny colour and he wore his hair short back and sides with a fringe flicked across his forehead. It was love at first sight.'

'Was he tall?'

'Yes, a lovely build too. I was the envy of all the girls.'

'I'd love to meet him but I suppose you have no idea where he lives.'

'I don't. Although...'

'What?'

'When my sister and I were clearing out the house after our father died, I found a letter addressed to me. Unfortunately, the contents had been ripped off but there was an address. That could be a starting point for you to track him down.'

'Will you help me?'

'As much as I can. Yes.'

I checked the time on my watch. 'Oh my god, it's four o'clock. I promised Mum I'd be home for tea plus I need to get ready to go out with my boyfriend this evening.'

'You have a boyfriend?'

'Yes.' Butterflies swarmed in my stomach at the thought of him. 'But I must go. I'll tell you about him another time.' I picked up my coat and rose from the bench.

Peggy followed me. 'I'll walk you to the bus stop. That way you can tell me about your young man.'

'Okay.' As we hurried along the pathway I said, 'His name's Joe and he's awfully dishy.'

'Enough said. Maybe I'll get to meet him further down the line. That is if you're still together.'

'I think we're for keeps.'

'Are you being careful?'

'We've not done anything like that... If that's what you mean. I'm keeping myself until my wedding night and Joe respects that.'

'I can see you have your head screwed on properly.'

'I just listened to my mum. And she's right. It'll be all the more special if we wait.' I stopped at the shelter. 'The bus should be here in a minute. Oh, here it is now.' The green double-decker pulled into the lay-by. 'We could meet Tuesday afternoon if you like? I'll take a day's holiday. Twelve o'clock at the clock tower?'

'Perfect. Until then, Rachel.'

'Christine, remember.' I smiled, stepped up to the platform, and turned back to wave. I liked Peggy and I liked being Christine.

I closed the front door.

'Is that you, Rachel?' Mum called.

I ambled into the kitchen. 'Yes, Mum, but I forgot to tell you that I'm going out to eat this evening. Would it be okay if I just grabbed a bit of a snack?'

'If that's all you want. Help me get this lot onto the table.'

I carried bowls of homemade potato salad and coleslaw into the dining room. Mum really did make the best. She followed me in with a basket of fresh bread rolls and a platter of cheese and ham.

'So, while we're alone,' Mum said, 'would you like to tell me who's taking you out to dinner?' Her eyes glinted.

I wondered whether I should tell her but instead said, 'Just a friend.'

'And do I know this friend?'

I smiled. 'No, not yet.'

She patted me on the arm. 'I hope we get to meet him soon.'

Jenny swayed into the room. 'Get to meet who soon?'

I touched my nose. 'Mind your own.'

Jenny scowled. 'Are you meeting her again tonight? You are, aren't you?'

'No, I'm not.' She'd guessed I was meeting my mother earlier but I'd no intention of letting her know that Peggy was taking me shopping next Tuesday.

'Who then? Who's this mystery person?' Jenny probed.

'Why are you so interested in my life? Get your own.'

'I see it's a normal Webster teatime.' Dad leaned over and pecked Mum on the cheek.

'She won't tell us who she's meeting tonight, Dad.'

Mum set the plates on the table. 'Leave your sister alone, Jennifer.'

'Exactly. Leave me alone.' I buttered a brown bread roll, added a slice of cheddar cheese and spooned out a serving of coleslaw and potato salad onto the side of my plate.

Dad piled salad onto his plate. 'Where are you off to this evening, Rachel?'

'I'm going to that new Italian restaurant in town. The Lime Bistro. Have you been there?'

'Yes, I was there last week on a business meeting. I must take your mother. You'd like it, Rosalind.'

Mum put down her knife and fork. 'That would be lovely. We haven't been out for a while and it would be nice to have a reason to dress up. What are you planning to wear, Rachel?'

'I thought I'd wear the little black shift that I bought last week.'

68

'That sounds beautiful. My little girl is all grown up. I tell you what, you can borrow my pearl choker. It's on my dressing table.'

'Thanks, Mum. Sorry, but will you excuse me? Only I need to run a bath or I'll be late,' I added as I got up from the table.

'Come and see us before you go,' Dad shouted after me. What he meant was he wanted to check the length of my skirt.

I stood at the full-length mirror swaying. The dress fitted me like a glove. Plain black georgette, sleeveless and a low neck, but not so low that Dad could complain. He'd not be able to find fault with the length either as it was only just above my knee. My hair looked gorgeous too, the dark brown showed red tints under the light. I stepped into my three-inch black stilettos. Joe had passed his driving test last week and had arranged to borrow his dad's car so we didn't have to go on the bike.

'Mum,' I called, 'where did you say I'd find the choker?'

'On my dressing table but don't worry, I'll come up.'

Before I knew it Mum was in my room. 'Here it is. Turn around and I'll fasten it for you.'

I ran my fingers across the black velvet cameo choker. 'It's perfect. Thank you.'

'Let me look at you.' Mum turned me around to face her. 'You look stunning. You just need a little bit of blusher and lipstick. Hang on one moment.' She darted out of my room into hers, and was back in seconds with a flowery cosmetic bag in her hand. She unzipped the pouch and took out a tiny case. After dabbing a brush across it she smoothed it over my cheeks, across my nose and under my eyes. 'There that's better. You now have a sun-kissed appearance. Now for a bit of lipstick.' She filled my lips in with an almost nude colour, giving me a natural look.

She'd never been like this with me before. Did she feel threatened about Peggy? Was I being fair? 'Thanks, Mum.'

'You're welcome, now go and say goodbye to your dad before you go.'

'All right.' I headed downstairs and into the lounge. 'What do you think?'

My dad glanced up. 'You look very sophisticated. Don't be home too late.'

'I won't.' I sensed a warm glow across my face. Mum and Dad seemed to really care about me. I felt a little guilty getting to know Peggy but she was Peggy, and Mum and Dad were Mum and Dad.

Joe was leaning against the car when I reached him. 'I heard clip clopping,' he said, 'thought it must be you. You look fabulous but you must be freezing. He took off his jacket and put it around my shoulders.'

'Thanks.' I climbed into the vehicle, smelling the newness from the leather. 'This is nice. A Cortina 1600E?'

'Yeah. My dad's new toy.'

'I'm surprised he let you borrow it when you've only just passed your test.'

Joe started up the engine. 'He knows I'll take good care of it, but he did make me promise not to drink.' He flicked the indicators to turn left off the roundabout. 'It's just down the road here.'

He was wearing Brut again. If he hadn't been driving, I'd have snogged him there and then. A light blue Ben Sherman shirt and camel-coloured flared trousers replaced his normal jeans and sweater. I was lucky to have him as my boyfriend.

Joe pulled up outside a picturesque restaurant with a blue-striped canopy over the window. He got out of the car, came around to the passenger side, and opened my door. 'M'lady.' He took my hand.

'Thank you, Parker.'

We laughed.

'Remember this is my treat.' Joe picked up the menu.

I knew better than to argue with him when he was forceful like that. Over the last six months I'd made sure he hadn't paid for everything. It wasn't fair when he was only working part-time and I was full.

He peered over the menu, his dark brown eyes sparkling. 'You look spectacular. How did I get to be so lucky to grab a great chick like you?'

'You don't scrub up so bad yourself.' I chuckled.

'What do you fancy?'

I shrugged my shoulders. 'You order for us both.'

'Okay. Do you like pizza?'

'I don't know. I've never tried it.'

'Neither have I' – Joe stroked his smooth chin – 'let's give it a go.' He caught the attention of a waiter hovering near the table. 'We'll have two seven-inch margheritas and a bowl of green olives, please.'

'Certainly, sir. And drinks?'

Joe looked at me.

'Just a lemonade.'

'Two lemonades.' He closed the menu and handed it to the waiter. I passed mine too.

'Thank you, sir.'

As he disappeared a young waitress appeared and lit the candle in the centre of our table.

'Thank you,' I said.

She smiled before leaving.

'This is lovely, Joe. So romantic. Thank you.'

He reached for my hand. 'I want it to be a special occasion.'

'For what? Have I forgotten something?'

'No. All will be revealed shortly.'

The girl was back with our drinks. 'Two lemonades. Your meal will be here shortly.'

Joe lifted his glass and clinked it with mine. 'Cheers.'

I picked up mine and clinked his back, careful to avoid the dancing flame. 'Cheers.' My heart was pounding. Joe looked so handsome. His dark-brown hair shone, brushing his shoulders.

The waiter returned and set down a golden pizza in front of each of us. I cut into mine and took a bite. 'It's delicious.'

'Yum. It is.' He held up his hand and the next thing I knew there was a string trio at our table, one playing a cello and the other two violins. They were joined by a woman singer with almost black hair. I was being serenaded although I couldn't understand the song as it was in Italian.

Joe beamed.

'You arranged this?'

He grinned.

I wasn't sure whether my butterflies were from excitement or embarrassment as the customers at other tables looked across, whispering and smiling.

Once the musicians had finished, the whole restaurant applauded them. They moved over to another couple at the back. Joe rose from the table, dug into his trouser pocket, and kneeled on the floor. 'Rachel, I know we've not known each other for long but you know how I feel about you. I've known since the first moment we met. I love you. Will you marry me?'

Burning up, I covered my face. My pulse, I was sure, had trebled. 'I love you too but...'

He got up off the floor and back into his seat. 'You're not going to say no, are you?'

'No. I'm not, but how can we get married when we're so young? You've not even met my parents yet and I've not met yours.'

'I know, but we can do that in time. I'm not expecting us to get married for a couple of years but I just want the world to know that you're my chick.'

'All right then. Yes, yes, I will but... You're not just asking me because...'

'No. I'm not trying to get you into bed. I told you, I'm happy to wait.' He put a hand across his chest. 'My heart's banging like a drum.' He slid a small diamond ring onto my finger.

Chapter Thirteen

Peggy

Adam put down his knife and fork on the plate, took a swig of coffee, and grabbed a piece of toast as he got up. 'Gotta go, love, else I'll be late. Thanks for a lovely brekkie.' He kissed me leaving crumbs on my lips. 'Sorry about that.' He laughed. 'Oh, I almost forgot to ask. Have you got any plans today?'

'Yes, I'm meeting Rachel. We're going shopping first and then I've booked us in for lunch at a nice restaurant.'

'Have a lovely time. Must go. Sorry.' He hurried out of the kitchen.

The front door slammed and the car engine started up. I peered out of the window as he drove off. I was lucky to have Adam. He supported me in everything. Collywobbles filled my stomach from excitement at the thought of meeting Rachel today, and doing girlie things together, like Kate and I had done many a time. Maybe one day in the not-too-distant future it would be the three of us going on a shopping trip.

Kate rushed into the kitchen.

'Morning, darling. Sit down and I'll get you breakfast.'

'No time, Mam. I'm late.'

'But, Kate...'

'Don't start. None of my friends eat breakfast.'

'Maybe they can cope with losing a bit of weight.' I tutted.

'Here. I'll take this.' She grabbed a rosy apple from the fruit bowl. 'Satisfied?' She took a bite and fled from the house. Kate had been picking at her food lately. She was at that age worrying about her figure, but she was losing too much weight. I was sure of it. It definitely wasn't the time to tell her she had an older sister.

After clearing the dishes from the table, I washed up quickly, leaving them on the drainer to dry. I had to put Kate to the back of my mind so I could concentrate on Rachel. I wiped my hands down my pinny, took it off, and threw it into the laundry basket.

⤙⚘

Rachel was at the clock tower when I arrived. She looked stunning in a white polo top that set off her dark hair, paired with a black and grey tartan kilt about two inches above her knees.

'You look nice?' I kissed her on the cheek.

'Ta.'

'Shall we shop first or have a coffee?'

Her eyes sparkled. 'Shop.' She grinned. 'If that's okay with you?'

'Perfect. I thought we'd start with Designer Lance to find you a handbag.'

'Wow. Thanks.'

After making our way up the High Street, we stopped at the traffic lights opposite the shop and waited for them to turn red before crossing the road. A bell dinged as we entered the store. Rachel scanned the area. 'That's what we want.' She headed for a shelf full of various handbags, picking up a black patent leather similar to mine. 'What do you think?'

I lifted a John Romain tweed with brown leather from the lower shelf. 'I know you wanted one like mine but this seems more suited to your age. It will be perfect for the summer.'

Rachel unflicked the gold clasp and checked the inner purse. 'It's nice but...'

'You'd set your heart on the patent leather?'

'Yep. Is that okay?'

Twenty-five pounds for the patent was a tenner more expensive than the reduced tweed. I'd specifically chosen this shop because they had a sale on. I chewed my lip. 'If that's the one you like, then that's the one we'll get.'

'Thanks Peggy.' Rachel handed the bag to the mature sales assistant standing by her side. 'We'll have this one, please?' Next thing she rushed over to the boots. 'Look at these white boots? They're so groovy and in the sale.'

The assistant smiled and turned to me. 'The matching white bag is in the sale too. For the same price as this black one she could have the boots and matching bag.'

'May I try the boots, Peggy? Please?'

'Yes, okay.'

Rachel checked the inside of the boots for sizing. 'Size 6.' She unfastened her chunky heeled black leathers and stepped into the white stretch, vinyl knee boots. They did look nice. Really finished off the outfit she was wearing and after all it wasn't going to cost me any more money if she opted for the white bag too.

The assistant headed our way with the white bag. 'Try it. The shoulder bags are all the rage for you youngsters.'

'That'll be a perfect match,' I said, praying she'd agree.

Rachel put the strap over her shoulder and made for the mirror. She swayed either side. 'My friend Linda's going to be so green.'

'Does that mean you'd like them?' the assistant asked.

Rachel turned to me with a pleading look.

'It looks like you have a sale,' I said.

'Come this way.' The assistant headed over to the counter and wrapped the items in tissue before placing them in a carrier bag displaying the shop's name. 'That will be twenty-five pounds exactly.'

I handed over my Barclaycard. What was I going to say to Adam? It was no good. I needed to get a job if I was going to be treating my firstborn to expensive stuff. Bless her, Kate would have gone for the cheapest item in the shop, knowing that her dad and I couldn't afford much but I supposed Rachel was used to her parents spending lavishly on her. Twenty-five quid would be nothing to them.

The assistant put my card through the machine. 'If I can just get you to sign.' She pushed the form forward that she'd marked with a cross.

After signing, I handed it back and she gave me the top copy along with my card. Adam wouldn't mind me spending all that cash, I tried to convince myself. Especially as I'd managed such a bargain. 'Are you ready?' I asked Rachel.

'Yes. Thanks.' She brushed her lips across my cheek and meandered out of the shop swinging the paper bag at her side. 'Linda's going to be so jealous.' She beamed.

'I'm glad you're happy. It can be an early birthday present. Do you have anything planned this weekend?'

'Who knows?' She shrugged. 'Maybe I'll see Joe. Where are we going for coffee?'

'I thought we might have some lunch. I've reserved a table at the Berni Inn just up the road.'

'Cool.'

We crossed the road opposite the Farmers Arms and pushed the door open into the steakhouse. A waiter approached. 'Do you have a reservation, madam?'

'Yes. A table for two in the name of Davies.'

He studied the appointment diary. 'Davies. Half past one. Table for two.' After ticking us off in the book he picked up two menus. 'Come this way.'

We followed him across to a window booth. 'I hope this is suitable.'

'Perfect, thank you.' I slid across the front facing bench and Rachel sat opposite, placing her carrier bag on the seat next to her. 'What are you having?' she asked.

I browsed the menu searching for the cheapest option. 'I thought perhaps plaice and chips.' Luckily ice cream or cheese and biscuits for dessert came as part of the price.

'Far out.' Rachel perused the options. 'Would you mind if I had rump steak? It comes with chips.'

It was another twenty-nine pence on top of the plaice. *Stop it, Peg, you invited your daughter for a meal so don't be so bloody tight.* 'Have whatever you like, Rachel.'

'You mean Christine.'

'To be honest I think Rachel suits you better.'

The waiter was at the table. 'Are you ready to order?'

I nodded. 'One plaice and one rump steak, please. Both with chips.'

He wrote our order down on his little pad. 'How would madam like the steak cooked?'

'Well done, please.' Rachel closed the menu and passed it to him. I did the same.

'And drinks?' The waiter looked from Rachel to me.

'Orange juice please.' Rachel smiled.

'Two orange juices then, please.' I was adding up the cost in my head.

Once the waiter had left Rachel said, 'This will be my second special meal this week.'

'How come?'

'Well, you know I was meeting my boyfriend last Sunday?' Her brown eyes glinted.

'You did mention that. You also said you'd tell me all about him today.'

Rachel's smile widened. She pulled out a necklace from under her jumper and held up a diamond ring on the chain. 'He proposed.'

'Really? And you said yes?'

'I did.'

I squinted. 'I'm a little confused if you said *yes* why isn't the ring on your finger? Does it need resizing? We could find a jeweller today if you like.'

'The size is perfect but I've not told my family yet. You're the only person I've told besides my best friend.'

'I'm honoured.' I fiddled with my own rings. She was seeing me more like a friend than a mother but who could blame her? I'd have to make do with that for now.

'Did you bring the letter with the address?'

'I did.' I opened my bag and handed over the airmail envelope.

Rachel unfolded it and studied the contents. 'America. I can't believe he lives in America.' She pushed it back to me. 'But will you write? I think it would be better coming from you than me. After all, does he even know I exist?'

'No. He doesn't. You're right. I'll write for you but please don't get your hopes up too much because there's no guarantee he still lives there.'

'I won't. But we've got to try, haven't we?'

'There's something else I think you'll like.' I passed her the black and white photograph of Mike and me.

'Is this him?'

'Yes.'

'Wow. You weren't exaggerating when you said he was good-looking. Can I keep it?'

The thought of giving it up made my head spin but I should never have kept it in the first place. It was disloyal to Adam. 'Yes, of course. That's why I brought it.'

'Thanks, Peggy.' She continued to stare at the picture.

'And you'd better have these.' I handed her a batch of envelopes. 'The birthday cards I bought each year for you from your first birthday.'

'Thank you.' She fingered the top one. 'Shall I open them now?'

'It's up to you, but you might like to keep them until later.'

'Yes, that's a much better idea.' She picked up the bundle of cards and popped them into the carrier bag with her gifts.

'So, tell me, are you planning to go to university?'

'No. Why do you ask? You know I have a job.'

'I thought perhaps Woolies was temporary.'

'Well, it isn't.'

'Oh.'

Rachel's face reddened. 'What do you mean, oh?'

'I'd rather hoped you'd have had a better start in life.'

'You sound like my mum and dad.'

'I can understand if they're not happy. Why Woolies?'

'Cos, I like it there. Isn't it more important to be happy than having a posh job? I suppose you'd rather I was a nurse or something like that?'

'I didn't say that.' I blinked. 'I'm just surprised, but if you're happy...'

She folded her arms. 'Well, I am.'

A waitress came to our table armed with two meals. 'Rump steak?'

Rachel put her hand up and the young woman set the plate down in front of her. She turned to me. 'And you must be the plaice.'

'Yes, thank you.'

We ate our meal in silence. I'd blown it. I wasn't sure what to say or how to mend the situation. 'How's your meal?' I asked.

'Good, thanks.' She tucked into the steak.

Adam came behind me and put the dirty dishes next to the sink. 'I'll wipe.' He picked up the tea towel.

'Thanks.' I placed the plates into the hot soapy water.

'You okay, Peg? You were quiet over dinner.'

'I'm fine.' I blinked to stop tears as I rinsed the final dish.

'No, you're not.' Adam threw the tea towel onto the table and turned me around to face him, gently pressing his fingers on my shoulders. 'What's up?'

'Nothing.'

'How did today go?'

I turned to the door to see if the kids were about.

'They're not here. Neil's gone out and Kate's up in her room. Come and sit down.' He guided me to a dining chair.

'I blew it.' The held back tears flowed.

'What do you mean?'

'Everything was going well. I treated her to a new handbag and a pair of boots and then we went to the Berni for lunch.'

'Bloody hell, Peg. How much did you spend?'

'Not a lot. They were in the sale and let's face it, Adam, I owed her that for all the birthdays and Christmases I've missed.'

'Yeah, okay. What happened?' He poured out two teas and handed me a mug. 'Here.'

'You know she works at Woolies? All I said was I rather hoped she'd have had a better start in her life than that.'

'Well, yes, I got the impression her parents were well off.'

'They are. She said it was more important for her to be happy than have a good job. She's right of course. What right do I have to an opinion? She's engaged too.'

'Really?'

'Yes, but her parents don't know about it yet. She was wearing the ring on a chain around her neck.' I put my hands to my face. 'Oh Adam, what am I going to do if she doesn't want any more to do with me. I was looking forward to girlie days out, not just with Rachel, but Kate too. And I wanted her to meet Kate and Neil and become part of our family.'

Adam patted me on the arm. 'Maybe that was a fairy tale world, Peg. Try and not think about it.' He slapped his thighs. 'Tell you what, Mrs D, let's go for a wander and pop in The Black Jug for a pint. What do you say?'

I sniffled, wiping a handkerchief across my eyes before blowing my nose. 'I'll just go and fix my face.'

'That's my girl.' He pecked me on the cheek.

Chapter Fourteen

Rachel

My feet were killing me. It had been all go at work this morning. School mums coming in to buy sweets to stuff in mugs or to decorate cakes for the local school fayre. I'd been hard on Peggy on Tuesday, especially after she'd spent all that money on me for the boots, handbag, and lunch. I could see she was calculating in her head whether she could afford them or not, and then I went in a mood just because she thought I should go to university.

A tap on the glass counter broke my thoughts. I gazed up at a woman in a black raincoat and paisley headscarf.

'Yes, madam, what can I get you?'

She sniffed, rubbing her nose. 'Give us three lots of two ounces of those jazzies for the kids' – she pointed to the chocolate buttons covered in hundreds and thousands – 'and a quarter of pineapple chunks for me.' The woman chuckled.

'Certainly.' I scooped the jazzies into three small paper bags and weighed them one by one. Afterwards I did the same with the pineapple chunks, adding an extra couple to get the correct weight, twirled the bags closed and passed them over.

She handed me a pound note. I rang up the confectionary on the till, put the pound note in the drawer and gave her the change.

'Ta.' The woman popped a sweet in her mouth as she left.

I glimpsed at the clock. Lunchtime, thank God. I needed to rest my feet for a bit. At this rate I wouldn't be able to wear my new boots this evening.

Mrs Davies waddled over. 'Wanna go for lunch, pet?'

'Yes, please.' I hobbled from behind the counter and across the shop towards the staffroom. Once I was out of view of the customers, I slipped my shoes off and climbed the stairs in my stocking feet. Someone nudged me in the back. I turned around to see Linda. 'Oi, that hurt.'

'What's the matter with you, grumpy guts?' She pushed the door open into the staffroom.

'I've been run ragged all morning. The world's gone mad. Just because it's the bloody school fete this Sunday.'

'Want a cuppa?'

'Yeah. Thanks.' I opened my locker, took out my sandwich box and lifted the lid. Cheese and pickle on brown. My favourite although I had no appetite. 'What have you got?' I asked on sitting down.

Linda unwrapped the greaseproof paper. 'Potted beef again. I wouldn't mind one of yours.'

'Help yourself. I'm not that hungry anyway.' I wondered whether I should tell her about my mother. 'Lind...'

'What is it?'

I chewed my lip. 'If I tell you something, promise to keep it to yourself?'

'You know I will. We're best friends. What is it?' She took a bite of the sarnie.

I glanced at the door to make sure no one was coming in.

'You're all right. We've got the room to ourselves. No one else has lunch at this time today. You can speak freely. Go on...' She put her hand over her mouth. 'You haven't, have you? You have.'

'No. No, it's nothing like that. You know we needed our birth certificates for the passports.'

'That was ages ago. Have you not had yours yet? Not that there's any rush now we've decided to go in October.'

'Yes. I got mine but it's not that.' I took a sip of tea.

'What then? Spit it out.'

'I'm adopted.'

'No way,' she shouted in a crescendo.

'Shh. Yes.'

'Your Jenny too?'

'Nope, just me. Anyway, I've been meeting up with my real mother.'

'And you're only telling me now?'

'I know. I'm sorry but I didn't want anyone to know. I've not even told Joe. It made me feel less of a person. You know... my mother not wanting me. Well, it turns out she had no choice. It seems her father sorted out the adoption and she got no say.'

Linda spluttered on her sandwich. 'You're kidding me.'

'Nope. Anyway, on Tuesday I went shopping with her.'

'Wow. Get anything nice?'

'Yes. Peggy, that's my mother's name, took me to Designer Lance, you know the designer bag and shoe shop in the High Street?'

'I know it, but never been inside. Far too expensive. Is she loaded then?'

'No, quite the opposite, but she must have felt guilty for giving me up because she bought me a pair of those white PVC boots I've wanted for ages, and a matching handbag.'

'You lucky cow.'

'I know but...' I sighed.

'What?'

'We went to the Bernie for lunch and all was going well until I told her where I worked and she started being judgemental about my job. I think I overreacted. I was horrid to her. Didn't even bother saying goodbye properly or thank her for the presents she'd bought me. I was a cow, Lind. Now I'm not sure what to do.'

'Simple. You tell her you're sorry.'

'Suppose she's not interested. Probably thinks I'm a spoilt brat which maybe I am.'

'Gawd you're a dark horse. How long have you known for?'

'Since November.'

'What?' She almost flew off her chair. 'I can't believe that you're only just telling me now.'

'Calm down. I've known about it since November but I only met her a couple of weeks ago.'

'Do you know where she lives?'

'Yes.'

'Then maybe you should go round her house after work and apologise?'

'No, I don't want to do that because she's got other kids.'

'You've got brothers and sisters?'

'Yep. One of each but she hasn't told them about me yet. All a bit early and after my outburst on Tuesday she probably wants nothing else to do with me. I bet she's glad she gave me away.'

'Stop feeling sorry for yourself. Write her a letter or is she on the phone?'

'She's on the phone.'

'Then ring her after work.' Linda looked at her watch and slapped my lap. 'Come on you, we'd best get back downstairs.'

I slipped on my new boots and checked the mirror; they looked real cool with my black tartan kilt showing my slim legs from a couple of inches above the knee. Even Dad wouldn't be able to complain about me displaying too much flesh. After spraying Gingham behind my ears and on my pulses, I lifted my wrist to smell. Gorgeous. If Joe wore Brut this evening our fragrances would meld as they were so similar. In fact, next time I planned to buy Brut because it was cheaper.

Ready to go, I hurried downstairs and unhooked my leather jacket off the peg. 'Bye,' I yelled.

'You look nice,' Mum said as I was heading out of the front door.

'Thanks, Mum.'

She lowered her head to my feet.

'When did you get them?'

'I bought them the other day.'

'But I thought you had no money. You were asking your dad for some. Got a magic money tree?'

'If you must know...'

Dad was in the hallway. 'What's going on? You off out again?'

'Yes, and if that's the end of the Spanish inquisition I need to go before I'm late.'

'No, Rachel, it isn't.' Mum frowned. 'Where did you get the money from for the boots? That girl hasn't got you shoplifting, has she?'

'She'd better not have.' Dad raised his voice. 'Answer your mother now.'

'If you must know Peggy bought them for me. And this too.' I swished the bag on my shoulder.

Mum scratched her nose. 'I didn't think she was well off. How did she afford to buy you designer stuff?'

'There was a sale on. And she bought me them because you and Dad wouldn't.'

Mum shook her head. 'I don't know what's got into you, girl. I hope you're not manipulating that woman to make her feel guilty.'

'It's got nothing to do with you. That's between her and me and if you don't mind, I'm going to be late.' I opened the front door.

'Rachel, don't you dare walk out that door,' Dad said.

After stepping over the threshold, I slammed the door. I'd worry about Mum and Dad later. If they didn't like how I was then I'd stay with Linda. I hurried down the road. Joe was waiting and wolf-whistled as I approached.

'Cor, I'm one lucky bloke.'

'Thanks.' I pecked him on the lips and climbed behind him on the pillion.

He rode into Woodhaerst via country roads and parked up in the car park of The Six Bells next to St James, a beautiful old Saxon church. 'We can get married there if you like?'

Married? I hadn't given getting married any thought. I'd accepted his proposal but was thinking marriage would be years off. I wasn't ready for all that housewife drudgery and a horde of kids. I just chuckled. 'Plenty of time to think about that. Let's go and find the others.'

Joe took my hand as we entered the pub. Linda was waving like mad near the dartboard. 'Over here you two.'

We bustled through the noisy crowd around the smoky bar until we reached Linda and Stu.

'Wow. Those boots are cool.' Linda marched backwards and forwards a few paces singing, 'These boots are made for walkin.'

'They're really comfy too.'

'How are your feet now?'

'Fine after a good soak in the bath.'

Linda dropped the darts on the table, and seated herself down, pulling me next to her. 'You really do look fab. I'm envious.'

I smiled, feeling myself heating up. 'I didn't enjoy work today.'

'At least we've got a day off tomorrow. A nice long weekend.'

'I know, but I've been thinking. Maybe Woolies isn't where I want to be. I'm going to try and get a job as a secretary or something.'

'You're not going to leave me?'

I shrugged my shoulders. 'I'm bored. You should sign up for evening classes to learn to type. That way you can get a job in an office too.'

Linda scowled. 'Shut up about it now. The boys are back with the booze.'

Chapter Fifteen

Rachel

I tapped Linda on the shoulder. 'Ta-ra then.'

'You not waiting for me?'

'Sorry, our Jen's waiting,' I lied. 'I'll see you tomorrow.'

'Charmed I'm sure.' She frowned. 'Suit yourself.'

I'd arranged to meet Peggy at three o'clock but first I had an interview with The Echo as a receptionist/shorthand typist. I didn't want to mention it to Linda because I knew she'd try and change my mind. Woolies was fun at first but not anymore. I was bored out of my skin, hated the standing up all day, and I wanted my Saturdays off.

I rushed across to the newspaper office and was greeted by a bald-headed man behind the counter. 'Good afternoon, miss. How can I help you?' He repositioned his round-rimmed spectacles across the bridge of his nose.

'I've an appointment with Mr Strange at quarter past one.'

'Ah, that's me. You must be Miss Webster?'

'Yes, yes, I am.'

He came out from behind the counter and turned the sign on the door to CLOSED. 'Take a seat.' He signalled to a small table and chairs.

'Thank you.' My pulse hammered. This was the first proper interview I'd had. I couldn't count Woolies as I was a Saturday girl first and they didn't even ask me any questions.

Mr Strange picked up a pen. 'So, Miss Webster, tell me why you think you'd be suitable for this position.'

'I like working with members of the public.'

'I see. And what experience have you had?'

'I've been working full time at Woolworths since September and prior to that I worked there as a Saturday girl for two years.'

He sneered when Woolworths was mentioned but I stayed calm and smiled waiting for the next question.

'Have you got any typing qualifications?'

'Yes. I have RSA I with credit, RSA II and III with distinction.'

He stroked his greyish goatee. 'I'll need you to do a typing test. How do you feel about that?'

'Not a problem.' I hoped I could still type with the speed and accuracy I'd had at college.

'Very well. Follow me.' I followed him down the corridor into a small office. 'Take a seat here.'

I lowered myself onto the office chair in front of an Olivetti typewriter. Mr Strange passed me a card with a page of text. I fed a piece of A4 paper into the machine, and set the margins.

'Ready?' he asked.

I nodded.

He pressed the button on his stopwatch and I began typing, relaxing as I remembered where the keys were.

After around five minutes he pressed the button on the timer and shouted, 'Stop.'

I stopped, waiting for his next instruction.

'Let me take a look.'

I pulled the paper release lever towards me, lifted out the sheet of paper and handed it to him. He studied it, nodding his head.

'Perfect. No errors at all. A good speed too. Sixty words per minute. How about your shorthand? There's a pencil and paper in the drawer next to you.'

I opened the drawer and took out the notebook. 'I'm ready.'

He picked up a newspaper and read out an obituary, a birth announcement, and an advert for a car. I scribbled down the symbols as I remembered.

'Now if you could type that up, please.'

I put in a fresh sheet of A4 and typed up my scribbles, pulled out the paper and passed it to him to inspect.

'This is excellent. When can you start?'

I smiled. 'I've got the job?'

'Yes, I don't see why not. A month's probation though.'

'Thank you. I'll need to give a week's notice.'

He flicked through a diary on the desk. 'Let's keep it nice and tidy. How about 22nd May? Two weeks this coming Monday.'

'Thank you.' I went to stand up.

'Don't you want to know more about the job and how much you'll get paid?'

I lowered myself back down. 'Yes, please.' I grinned.

'In the mornings you'll work back office. That could be typing from dictation or copy typing. You'll also be expected to use the switchboard. Have you ever used a switchboard?'

'No.'

'It's not hard.' He moved over to the side of the room where there was a board with eyelets and wires. 'Just five lines and ten extensions. Mrs Jones who works mornings will train you.'

I nodded.

He strode to the opposite side of the office. 'Did they teach you how to use a telex at college.'

I shook my head. 'But I'm a quick learner.'

'Mrs Jones will show you the ropes. She'll be your supervisor in the mornings. In the afternoons you'll be on reception and can come to me if you have any problems.'

'Thank you.' I clasped my hands together. There seemed to be a lot to learn. I hoped I was up to it.

'We'll pay you seven pounds fifty pence to start, and after one month's probation, if we're satisfied, it will rise to eight pounds. You'll also get seventy-five pence worth of luncheon vouchers a month.' He sniffed. 'How does that sound?'

'Brilliant, thank you.' That was more than I was getting at Woolies and I wouldn't have to work Saturdays.

'Excellent. We'll see you two weeks on Monday at half-past eight sharp. You'll be given an induction and introduced to the other members of staff then. Please wear a black suit with a white blouse. Do you own a black suit?'

'No.'

'Keep the receipt and you'll be reimbursed for two skirts, one jacket, and three blouses.'

'Thank you.'

'And don't forget to bring your P45 or you'll end up paying emergency tax. Off you go then. Welcome to the team.'

I stood up. 'Thank you, Mr Strange.'

'Oh, Miss Webster, turn the sign back to OPEN on your way out.'

'Will do.' I left the office and, once in reception, flicked the sign before banging the door shut. I'd got a new job and couldn't stop smiling. Although I wasn't sure how much I'd like working with Mr Strange. He definitely lived up to his name, but I'd get more pay and experience, and hopefully Mrs Jones and the other staff would be nice. All I had to do now was break it to Linda. She wasn't going to like it.

I checked the time on my watch. Ten past two. Enough time to buy Peggy a present if I could find a shop that wasn't closed.

Peggy was waiting under the clock tower when I arrived just before three o'clock. She looked around as if she was nervous. That was my fault. I strode up to her. 'Hello, Peggy.' I kissed her on the cheek. 'Thought we could go for a coffee. My shout.'

She smiled. Her body relaxed. 'That sounds nice. Where would you like to go?'

I wanted to avoid Elmo's in case Joe had finished college early and was on duty. 'How about Zig-Zag?'

'That works for me but you'll have to lead the way as I don't know that one.'

'It's not far,' I said.

We strolled around the corner. The town was quiet with half-day closing. 'It's just up the road now,' I said. 'How are you?'

'I'm fine thank you. And you?'

'I'm good. Really good. I've got a new job.'

'Really? Where?'

'At The Echo as an office assistant. Shorthand, typing, telex operator, telephonist and receptionist. A bit of everything.'

'Well done.' She beamed.

'The café's just over there.' I crossed the road with Peggy beside me. We wandered through the open entrance. 'Without You' was playing from the juke box. I loved that song. Peggy chose a table near the window. I took the seat opposite her and looked ahead at a guy in his forties, unshaven and red-eyed. He must've put the record on. Maybe he'd broken up with his wife. Or maybe she'd died? I hoped I'd never have to feel like that. 'Poor man,' I whispered to Peggy.

She squeezed my hand. 'Have you told your parents yet about your engagement to Joe?'

'No.' I tugged on the chain with the ring around my neck. 'They'll only spoil it. Anyway, never mind about that. I wanted to apologise for my behaviour at our last meeting.'

'That's all right,' she said as a plump woman waddled over to our table.

'What can I get yous?'

Peggy glanced at me. 'Coffee?'

'Yes, but I'm paying remember.'

She leaned back in her chair. 'Two coffees, please.'

Once the waitress had gone, I said, 'It's not all right. You spent all that money on me, and I knew you couldn't afford it, yet how did I repay you? By being a real cow. I'm sorry.' I dipped into my handbag. 'I bought you a present.' I handed her the gift-wrapped parcel.

'Thank you.' Her brown eyes sparkled as she ripped off the wrapping and opened the box. 'A cameo choker. It's beautiful.' She held the red velvet band to her slender neck. 'I love it. But...'

'But nothing. You deserve it and I promise not to treat you like that ever again. Well, I promise to try.' I giggled.

Jenny had already set out the table mats so I laid the cutlery and plates. The aroma of Mum's chicken casserole in the oven was making my stomach rumble. Jenny brought in a basket of jacket potatoes, brown and crispy, just the way I loved them. Using oven gloves, Mum carried in the flowery-patterned ovenproof dish and placed it in the centre of the table. She peered up at the clock. 'Six o'clock. Your father should be home any minute.'

In no time at all he'd pulled up on the drive. The car door slammed and I rushed to open the front door for him. 'Hello, Dad. Dinner's on the table.'

'Thank you, Rachel. You seem in good spirits.'

'I am, but I'll tell you about it over dinner.'

Dad took off his jacket and hung it up in the coat cupboard. 'Rosalind,' he called, 'I'm home.'

Mum hurried into the hallway and kissed Dad on the lips. They'd been married nearly thirty years yet they still seemed so much in love. I hoped that Joe and I would be like that.

Once we were all at the table, Mum served the casserole onto our plates, and we helped ourselves to potatoes.

'Rachel's bursting to tell us her news,' Dad said as he sprinkled salt and pepper on his meal.

I felt myself beaming. 'I've got a new job.'

'Oh?' Mum said. 'And where's this one?'

'Well, I think you'll be pleased.' I grinned. 'Working in The Echo office. A bit of everything really. Typing, shorthand, telephone. I start in a couple of weeks.'

Mum got up from the table and came and hugged me. 'That's wonderful news.'

'It really is,' Dad said, 'we're really proud of you. In fact' – he rose from his chair and moved over to the sideboard – 'I think we should celebrate.' He returned with four small crystal glasses and a bottle, and poured a drop of port out for each of us. Once we all had a glass Dad made a toast. 'To Rachel. Congratulations.'

Mum and Jenny echoed, 'Congratulations.'

'What was your day like, Jennifer?' Dad asked. 'Any special news?'

'I got an A-star for my latest assignment.'

'That's my girl.' Dad raised his glass again. 'And how about you, Rosalind, how's your day been?'

'Nothing special. A WI meeting this morning. What about you, Charles?'

'Quite mundane to be honest. Meetings all day. I'm glad to be home. Thought perhaps we could go for a wander around the park after dinner. Give my legs a bit of a stretch. Why don't you girls join us?'

'No thanks, Dad,' I said, 'I'm out with a friend this evening.'

'This wouldn't happen to be the same friend you've been out with before?' he asked.

I sensed myself blushing. 'It might be.'

'Why not invite him over to tea?' Mum said.

'I'm not sure we're ready for that yet.'

'It would be nice to see who our daughter's dating,' Dad said.

Jenny nudged me. 'Yes, bring him home.'

'I'll speak to him but I'm not making any promises.'

Chapter Sixteen

Peggy

I browsed through the classifieds in *The Echo* searching for a job. What could I even do? Perhaps go back to waitressing? After having Rachel I'd gone to London and got a job as a waitress. That's where I met Adam. Within four months of our meeting I was pregnant again. That time with Neil and there was no way my parents were going to stop me keeping that baby. I needn't have worried though because Adam was so excited about the news that he made arrangements for us to go to Gretna Green and we married almost straight away. I sighed. But it meant I only had around six months waitress experience; probably not sufficient. Maybe a job in a factory? A filing clerk? Yes, I could do that. A bit mundane but it would bring in a few bob. I circled an ad with details of an office temp agency; that way I could work the hours I wanted.

The post slipped through the letterbox. I put the newspaper down and went to the front door to pick up the letters. When I spotted the airmail envelope my stomach did somersaults. Trembling, I gripped the letter addressed to Peggy Davies. With an American postmark, it had to be from Mike. I made my way to the kitchen and switched the kettle on, wondering what was in the letter but too nervous to read it. My pulse thumped. I had no right to feel this way. I wasn't even sure why I did?

Steam filled the kitchen as the kettle boiled. I added a spoon of Nescafe into a mug and poured in the water. While my coffee was cooling, I headed to the hallway, picked up the telephone handpiece and dialled the number to the temp agency.

⁂

Adam went up to the bar. 'Here you go, Peg.' He placed half a lager and lime down on the table and a pint of bitter for him.

'Cheers.'

'I'm taking it that you'd like to talk about Rachel as you wanted to come out away from the kids?'

'In a roundabout way.' I took the airmail envelope from my handbag. 'Remember...' the rest of my sentence was lost in the roaring and shouting as someone scored one hundred and eighty in the darts match.

Adam picked up our drinks. 'Let's go into the saloon bar. There's no way we can have a conversation in here with that going on.'

I followed him through to the saloon where he selected a quiet booth at the back of the room. 'This will do.'

Once we were seated, he asked, 'Fancy trying again?'

I took a deep breath. 'You remember Rachel asked me to write to Mike using the address I had?'

'Yes, of course.' Adam took a packet of Embassy from his pocket, opened the box and passed it to me. 'Ciggy?'

'Yeah. Thanks. I picked one from the packet and Adam flicked his lighter for me to take a light. I took a drag from the cigarette and blew out a stream of smoke. 'Well, I got a letter back this morning.' I waved the envelope.

'He still lives there then?'

'No, but his sister did until recently. She'd left a forwarding address with the new owners who sent it on and she got in touch with Mike.'

'What does he have to say?'

'He was ecstatic to have heard from me and discover we had a daughter. He was married too but divorced last year.'

Adam flicked ash into the ashtray. 'Does he have any other children?'

The door opened and let a rush of cold air into the bar. 'That wind's picked up tonight.'

'Yes, it has. This weather's so unpredictable. So has he?'

'Has he what?'

'Any other children?'

'He didn't say. Do you fancy any crisps or nuts?'

'Not for me. You?'

'Nope. I'm fine. Still full from tea.' I took a sip from my drink.

'For Christ's sake, Peg, what did he say?'

'He says he'd love to meet Rachel and he can try to get over here or he's happy to send over two plane tickets to the States.'

'Two?' Adam frowned. 'Why two?'

I shrugged. 'I suppose he doesn't want her to go on her own.'

'Well, I hope he's not expecting you to go with her?'

'Of course not.' I turned my head away for a moment. 'Even if he does, naturally I wouldn't go. It wouldn't be right.'

'Too damn right it wouldn't be right. I support you in everything but that would be a step too far.' He swigged back the bitter and banged the empty pint glass down on the table. 'You ready. I think I'd rather be back at home.'

'Yes, sure.' I knew he wouldn't like it but he'd taken it a lot worse than I'd expected.

Chapter Seventeen

Rachel

Linda and I stood close to the manager as he locked up the shop.

'Goodnight, Miss Smith and Miss Webster. Have a good evening both of you.'

'Thank you, Mr Peters,' Linda and I answered in turn before he strode down the pavement.

'What's this about then?' Linda asked.

'I'll tell you when we get to Elmo's.'

'Did you sort that problem out with your new mam?'

'Yes, but I don't call her that. She's Peggy.'

'Oh, all right. Never mind that now, anyway. What's this about?' Linda asked again. 'I thought your mam liked you home in time for tea?'

'She does but I told her I'd be late as I need to speak to you.' The traffic lights turned red. 'Let's cross.'

'Are you seeing Joe this evening?'

'Not this evening. You seeing Stu?'

'Nope. I haven't seen him for days,' she said as we reached the cafe. 'I think he's going to chuck me.'

'Oh, Lind.' I put my arm around her shoulder. 'I hope not. Maybe he's got exams coming up or something?' How was I going to break the news to her now? But I had to. I pushed the door open and we wandered inside to our usual table.

Joe spotted us and came over. 'Hello, you two. I wasn't expecting to see you in here.'

'We needed a girlie catch-up.' I winked at him.

'Are you eating or just coffee?'

'We'll have a toasted teacake each please, and two coffees. You know how we like them.' I laughed.

'Be right back.'

Linda frowned. 'Are you trying to butter me up? Buying teacakes as well as coffee.'

'Of course not.' I blinked, hoping she wouldn't see right through me. 'I thought you'd be hungry. I know I am.'

She rubbed her stomach. 'You know me, I'm always starving. Thanks.' She slapped her hands on the table. 'Come on then, Webster, out with it. I know there's something.'

'Er... there is something but I don't think you're going to like it.'

Joe was back at our table and placed the coffees in front of us. 'Teacakes will be five mins.'

'Cheers.' I picked fluff from my jumper.

'Just get on with it, Rachel. Tell me. Are you cancelling our holiday?'

'No, of course not. Mind you we can hardly cancel something we haven't booked yet, but as far as I'm concerned we're still going away in October.'

'What then?'

'You know I didn't hang around after work yesterday?'

'Yes, I thought that was strange as you always wait for me.'

'I had an interview.'

'Interview? You mean for a job?'

'Yep. At The Echo.'

'You're leaving Woolies?'

'I got the job, so yes. It's working in an office. I start two weeks Monday. We can still meet up though at lunchtimes as I'll only be over the road.' I reached for her hand.

She pulled it back. 'You promised.'

'No, I didn't. I told you I was bored. I hate it there. I'm not like you, I don't want to be stuck there for years on end, even if I did get made a supervisor.'

'So, you think you're too good for it.' She scowled. 'I should've known. I hate you, Webster. You bring me out to butter me up and think a toasted teacake cuts it. Well, it doesn't. I've just told you that I think Stu's going to chuck me and then you make me even more miserable by telling me this. How could you?' She shot up from the seat. 'Stick your bloody teacake and stick your fucking friendship.' She charged out of the café.

I hurried after her. 'Lind, Lind, don't be like that. Please.'

She didn't turn back but picked up her speed and disappeared around the corner. I returned to the café and fell into the chair. Joe was by my side. 'What happened there?'

I shook my head. 'Well let's just say I wasn't expecting that. What time are you due a break?'

He peered up at the Roman numeral clock on the wall. 'I could take it now... if you like?'

'Yes, please.' I burst into tears.

He rubbed the top of my arm. 'I'll just clear it with the boss.'

I dabbed my eyes with a hanky. I hadn't expected her to take it well but, gawd, that was overreacting. Joe came back with the toasted teacakes. I pushed them away. 'I've lost my appetite but feel free to eat them.'

'Ta. I'm famished.' He bit into one of them. 'So, what happened?'

'You know I was going for that job yesterday?'

'Yeah. I've been wondering how you got on.'

'Well, I got it. And Linda got the hump because I'm leaving Woolies. What the hell does it matter? We can still see each other outside of work. Surely, we don't have to be in each other's pockets all of the time, do we?'

He reached across and took my hand. 'No, of course not. Good news about the job though. Congratulations. When do you start?'

'Two weeks Monday. It's more money and no Saturdays which means I can sleep in if I like.'

'Cool. I bet your folks were pleased?'

'They really were. They want to meet you by the way.'

'Wow. Really. And are you up for that?'

'Maybe. Perhaps you could come for tea one Sunday, but there's no rush.'

'Sure. I'd like that. Thanks.' He rubbed toast crumbs from his hands. 'Look, are you going to be okay, only...'

'Yes, I'll be fine. I'll get off home. I know you've got to get back to work. I'll see you tomorrow night.' I kissed him briefly on the lips.

When I reached the bus stop, Linda was leaning on the shelter. 'I'm sorry,' she said, 'I don't want us to fall out.'

'Come here.' I took her into a hug. 'This doesn't have to change anything between us. Why don't we go for a walk?'

'Okay.' Her stomach rumbled. 'I don't suppose you brought that teacake with you, did you?'

'Nope. Sorry. Joe ate them both.' I giggled. 'I'd lost my appetite, and you know Joe, he's like a human dustbin. Tell you what' – I signalled to the chippie – 'those chips smell awfully good. Why don't I treat us?'

'Sounds brill.'

We wandered into the empty chip shop. 'Two small bags of chips please,' I asked the grey-haired woman behind the counter.

'Be two ticks. Just finishing off cooking them so they'll be nice and fresh for you.' In no time at all she'd scooped up a portion each of the golden fries and wrapped them open, ready to eat.

We strolled into Maple Park tucking into our chips and stopped at a bench by a garden blooming red, yellow and pink roses. Once seated, I asked Linda, 'What's on your mind? I can't believe you got so stressed over me telling you about my new job.'

'Me mam...'

'What about her?'

'She's buzzed off again with her latest boyfriend. No idea when she'll be back. And Stu's going to chuck me, and you're going to leave me.'

'I'm not leaving you, Lind. We'll always be best mates. It's not like we see that much of each other at work, anyway. We're always too bloody busy. Surely as my friend you want me to be happy?'

She burst into tears.

'Hey.' I placed my bag of chips on the bench and put my arms around her. 'Come on, what's really bothering you?'

Linda pulled away and wiped her nose. 'I'm three weeks late. History repeating itself. My dad didn't want to know about me and now Stu's not interested in this one.' She put her hand on her stomach.

'How do you know Stu's not interested? And you don't even know yet whether you are?'

'I do. I'm never late. Last week I told him and I've not heard from him since.' She burst into tears again.

'Come on.' I let her sob on my shoulder.

Chapter Eighteen

Rachel

The doors closed at half past five as usual on my last day at Woolies. Mr Peters gathered all the staff around on the shop floor.

Gloria nudged me. 'Come on, kiddo, this is for you.'

I looked over at Linda, hoping for her support, as I sensed myself burning up from embarrassment. She turned her back on me, and made for the stairs but Gloria pulled her back. 'We've got the presentation. Did you forget?'

'Oh yes.' Linda scowled at me.

Mr Peters clapped his hands. 'All right, everyone. You know why we're here. It's to thank our youngest member of staff, Rachel Webster, who's made many of our dull days perkier by her warm smile. It's with great sadness that we see you go, Miss Webster, but we understand, you're young and need to make your life in pastures new.' He coughed to clear his throat. 'Your fellow workers made a collection to purchase you a gift which I have pleasure in presenting.' He passed me a small package and a white envelope.

'Thank you. I hadn't expected any of this.' I wiped my eyes. 'It's so very kind of you all.' I gave Linda a pleading glance but once again she turned away.

Gloria handed me a mixed coloured bouquet. 'Here you go, kiddo. Don't forget to come back in and see us.'

Sniffing the cornflowers, I answered, 'I won't.' Glaring at Linda, I said, 'You'll probably get fed up of seeing me as I'm only over the road.'

'Open your pressie,' came from the women in turn.

I tore the wrapping from the parcel, and pulled out a gold-plated pen set. 'This is lovely. Thank you.'

'And the envelope,' Mr Peters said.

I ripped it open. It was a good luck card and each person had signed it with a special message. But where was Linda's name? 'Lind?'

She ignored me. Gloria went over to my friend and took her into a hug. Linda burst into tears and ran upstairs to the staffroom.

Gloria patted my shoulders. 'She'll be okay.' She touched the envelope. 'There should be something else inside.'

I glanced at the door to the stairs.

'She can wait.' Gloria prodded me. 'Come on, open it up,' she whispered, 'the others have chipped in their hard-earned cash and want to see your face.'

All I wanted was to slip out without any fuss. I pulled out another card and inside was a five-pound record voucher. 'Wow. Thank you.' I hugged the members of staff in turn except Mr Peters, I shook his hand. This would buy a lot of records or maybe even an LP.

The staff in turn left the shop, all wishing me luck and saying goodnight to each other. Gloria stayed back. 'Go up and see your mate.'

I ran upstairs and found Linda sobbing.

'Oh, Lind.' I wrapped my arms around her. 'This isn't going to affect our friendship. I promise.'

She pushed me away. 'Fuck off to your poxy new job and leave me alone.'

'But Lind, you're my best friend.'

'Well, you're not mine. We're done. I hate you.' Barging past me she charged out of the staffroom and downstairs.

I didn't have the strength to try and catch her up. The whole day had been too emotional. What with it being my final day, the presentation, and Linda's behaviour. I wasn't even sure I knew who she was anymore.

It was eight o'clock in the morning when the bus pulled into town. Today was my first day at the new job and I needed to keep my mind off Linda. Yesterday I'd gone around to her house but she refused to answer the door. Hopefully in a few days time she'd calm down. It wasn't helping matters with Stu avoiding her. I'd speak to Joe about him later.

As I reached the door to The Echo, Mr Strange opened it. 'Good morning, Miss Webster. Nice and early, that's what we like to see.'

'Thank you.'

He checked out my black suit and white blouse. 'Yes, very presentable. You'll make a great ambassador when on the reception desk. Come and meet your colleagues.' He locked the door behind me and I followed him into the staffroom where a short, chubby lady was making tea.

'Listen up, everyone.' Mr Strange clapped his hands. 'This is Miss Webster, our new trainee. She'll assist Mrs Jones in the mornings, and in the afternoon once trained, she'll be on reception.'

The chubby lady waddled over to me. 'Welcome to the team. What's your first name?'

'Rachel,' I answered, my stomach curdling. Had I done the right thing? Supposing I wasn't up to the job?

'Don't look so worried,' the woman said. 'I'm Mrs Jones but you can call me Betty, and I'll look after you. We shan't expect you to go on the desk until you feel ready.' She ushered a girl over. 'This is Mel. Mel's secretary to John.'

Mel didn't look any older than me. Pretty with auburn hair in a long feather cut as if she'd just been to the hairdresser. 'Hi.' She smiled.

Betty beckoned over a tall bloke. 'This is John. He's our journalist, so he may need you to take dictation when Mel's off sick or on leave. And this is Sam our photographer. John and Sam are just off on a job.'

'Nice to meet you,' they answered in turn before shooting off.

Mr Strange peered up at the clock. 'It's five to nine so I must open up. I'll leave you in the good hands of Mrs Jones. Welcome to the team, Miss Webster.'

Once he'd gone, Betty introduced me to Mary, a filing clerk. Mary was in her thirties and worked part-time, nine to three, to fit in with her school children.

'Mel,' Betty asked, 'do you mind manning reception for the next couple of weeks while I train Rachel?'

'No. That's fine.' Mel picked up her handbag and went through to reception.

'Lizzie,' Betty said, 'is our normal morning receptionist but she's on annual leave. You'll get to meet her in a couple of weeks.' She shuffled over to the switchboard. 'Make yourself comfy.'

I took a seat next to her.

'Watch out for the light and buzz which show we have a call coming in. Stick the plug in the hole and flick this switch forward and answer, *The Echo, Miss Webster speaking, how can I help you?*' Betty shoved a notepad in front of me. 'Use this to write down their name and details, otherwise, believe you me, you'll forget. Especially when you have more than one caller on the line. Try putting the plug in and pushing the switch forward while listening in the earpiece.'

I did as she asked.

'What can you hear?'

'A dialling tone.'

'That's right. Oh look, that line's flashing. Take that plug out and plug in here and answer.'

I stuck the plug into the hole by the buzzing light and flicked the switch forward. My hands shook as I answered, 'The Echo. Miss Webster speaking. How can I help you?' I sighed with relief when it was Mel who answered. She told me she was ringing from reception as Betty had instructed her earlier.

'Well done.' Betty took the earpiece from me. 'Mary, can you come and man the switchboard, please?'

Mary put down a bunch of buff files on the desk and hurried over. 'Sure.'

Betty patted my hand. 'Don't worry, Rachel, we won't make you go solo until you're fully trained. I just wanted to hear how you sounded.' She smiled and I relaxed.

The morning went really quickly. I had a play on the telex, not transmitting anywhere, and I did a batch of copy typing.

'Go to lunch now,' Betty said, 'and I'll see you tomorrow as I only work mornings. This afternoon you'll be shadowing Mel on the reception desk. How have you found it so far?'

'Good. Although a little nerve-wracking but I think I'm going to enjoy working here.'

'That's what we like to hear.' She picked up her bag from under the desk. 'Bye, everyone,' she called and left the office.

'How did the job go?' Joe asked while we stood at the bar of The Six Bells waiting to be served.

'It was fun. I was so nervous though, but I did a bit of everything. Learned how to type on the telex, had a go on the switchboard, and did a huge batch of copy typing. Much better than Woolies.'

'A pint of Double Diamond for me and half a lager and lime for Rachel,' Joe said to Harry the landlord who knew us on a first name basis.

'Coming up.' Harry pulled on the pumps for Joe's drink, and took a bottle of Heineken from under the counter, trickled a drop of lime juice into a glass for me and poured in the lager.

'I'm paying,' Joe said, 'as we're celebrating your new job.' He passed a note to Harry who rang up the drinks on the till and gave Joe his change.

We picked up our glasses and made for a table close to the bar. Once we were seated Joe said, 'Your job sounds amazing. You did the right thing leaving Woolies and it's brought some peace at home with your parents.'

'Yes, you're right. I just wish Linda could see it that way. Did you get a chance to speak to Stu?' I sipped my lager and lime.

'No, I couldn't. He's not been at college since and when I phoned his house, his mam answered and said he'd gone to stay with his sister down south for a couple of weeks. Something to do with her needing him.'

'So, it sounds like he may have a legitimate reason for disappearing. Even so, he could have sent a letter or something. The last time I spoke to Linda she mentioned being late, you know? And she said she'd told Stu.'

'Nah, that doesn't sound like Stu. He'd stand by her. It's just a coincidence that he had to rush off.'

I shrugged my shoulders. 'I hope you're right.'

'Can you phone Linda and see if she's heard anything from him?'

'She's not on the phone and yesterday when I went around to her house, she wouldn't open the door.'

'Hmm, very strange. Anyway, never mind that, tell me more about your first day.'

Chapter Nineteen

Rachel

The telex sprang into life as it transmitted an incoming message. When it had finished, I ripped the paper from the roller and handed it to Betty.

After studying it she said, 'Take it through to Mr Strange as he may want to send a reply.'

'Okay.' I strolled down the corridor and knocked on the boss's door.

'Come in,' he called from the other side.

'Betty sent me in with this. It's just come through on the telex.'

He scanned the message. 'I'll work out a reply and bring it through later. While you're here, Miss Webster, take a seat for a moment.'

Smoothing the back of my skirt, to avoid crushing the linen fabric, I sank into the deep-cushioned chair opposite him. My knees trembled. Was he going to sack me?

He leaned back into his seat. 'I was wondering how you were getting on, as we're now into your third week?'

I smiled, breathing a sigh of relief. 'Very well, thank you. I love the job, and I'm learning so much.'

He nodded. 'That's good. Has Mrs Jones let you loose on your own to operate the telex and switchboard yet?'

'Yes. And today will be my first day flying solo on reception.'

'You're going to be an asset to this newspaper. In the future there will be plenty of career opportunities for you. Even the possibility of training as a journalist if you think that would be something that interests you.'

'Really? I had no idea.'

Mr Strange laughed. 'You keep going like you are and in a couple of years, maybe even a year, we can look at sending you on a journalist course.'

'Thank you. Thank you, Mr Strange.' I grinned.

He passed me his large orange mug. 'Be a good girl and bring your boss a nice cup of coffee.'

'Yes, of course.' I took the mug. There was no need to ask how he liked it as one of my jobs was to keep the team supplied with coffee and tea but I didn't mind at all. I closed the door behind me beaming inside as I meandered along the corridor to the back office. 'Anyone else for coffee? Tea?' I asked.

'Has his lordship got you making his tea again?' Betty laughed.

'Yes, only it's coffee. I don't mind though.' I flicked the switch on the kettle and added a heaped spoon of Nescafe to the mug. 'He said if I carry on like I'm doing I could train as a journalist in the future.'

Betty picked her bag up from under the desk. 'Is that what you want?'

'To be honest I'm not sure. I hadn't given it any thought but I've always loved writing so I think I would enjoy it. He said it won't be for a while but good to know there are career prospects.'

She patted me on the back. 'You're a quick learner, and a hard worker. Carry on like that and you'll go far. I'm off now. Finish making his coffee and then make sure you take your dinner break. Good luck on reception this afternoon. Don't forget Mel will be around if you have any problems.'

'Thanks, Betty.' The kettle boiled as she left. I poured water into the mug, added a dash of milk from the fridge, and gave the coffee a stir.

Mel came up behind me. 'I'll take it through if you like as I've got to go in and see him.'

'Thanks.'

'By the way, what are you doing at lunchtime tomorrow?'

'I'm not sure, why?'

'It's my birthday and we're all going across the road to the pub. Want to join us?'

'Yes, thanks. I'd like that.'

'Great.'

As she picked up the mug, I grabbed my bag from under the desk, and followed her down the corridor to leave the office. I'd made up my mind that I was going across to Woolies to catch Linda as it was Wednesday half day closing. I'd been in the shop a couple of times but she always made out she was busy so she didn't have to speak to me. Several times I'd visited her house but she never answered the door even though I knew she was in. I had to keep trying though because I wasn't ready to give up on our friendship.

Mr Peters was locking up the shop and Linda was close by. I ran across the road. 'Lind,' I called, but she turned and sprinted up the road. What was it with her? Was she pregnant and that's what was making her like this? I was seeing Joe this evening and I'd find out if he'd heard anything from Stu or not.

Joe revved the bike into The Six Bells car park. We climbed off and he took my hand as we strolled up to the pub entrance. 'I've missed you,' he said. 'Sorry I couldn't get the car tonight but Dad was taking Mum out. I think they needed a night out because they've been arguing a lot lately.'

'Oh? I hope they're okay. They're not getting a divorce, are they?'

'Bloody hope not. Think they're just going through a rough patch like all marriages do. I expect we'll row sometimes too. Wouldn't be normal otherwise.' He pushed the pub door open and I followed him in and up to the bar. 'The usual?' he asked me.

'Yeah, sure. I'll get the next round.'

'Good evening, lad and young lady,' Harry said. 'What can I get yous?'

'Half a lager and lime for Rachel, just a coke for me as I'm on the bike, and a pint of bitter for Stu.'

'Stu's here?' I asked him.

'Well, he will be. He's coming to chat about Linda.' Joe turned to the door. 'Here he is now.'

Stu swaggered over to the bar. 'Hiya Rachel. How you doing?'

I nudged his arm. 'You've got some nerve acting like you've done nothing wrong.'

'Well, I haven't.'

'She told me.'

'Told you what? Look let's wait until we've sat down and we can both share what we know.'

Joe stroked my arm. 'Come on, Rachel. Give Stu a chance. He's only come here this evening to try to help.'

'Very well, but it had better be good.' I picked up my drink, marched to the back of the room by the dartboard, and took a seat by the window. In no time at all Joe and Stu joined me.

'You're back then?' I said to Stu.

'Yeah. My sister split up with her husband and needed help moving into her new gaff.'

'How long had she been married?'

'Only a couple of years but he's an alcoholic and was coming home drunk from the pub and laying into her. I'm proud of her for having the strength to leave him.'

'I see. So, it had nothing to do with you disappearing after Linda told you she was late.'

'No, nothing. Honestly, Rachel, Linda has some serious issues.'

'Yep, she does. You breaking up with her when she needed you most.'

Stu took a box of Woodbines from his jacket pocket. 'Want one?'

'No thanks. I'd rather have an explanation why you let down my friend, your girlfriend, when she gave you that kind of news.'

Stu dangled a cigarette from his mouth and struck a match. 'It wasn't like what she said.' He took a drag.

'Then how was it?'

'She'd been getting more and more possessive. Wanting to know everything I was doing when I wasn't with her. Wanting to see me every night. I didn't want that. You don't complain about not seeing Joe all the time, do you?'

'No, of course not but then he has studying to do.'

'My point exactly. I have studying to do too but Linda wouldn't have that. She knows I have to study if I want to pass my exams but it didn't make any difference to her. She'd throw a tantrum every time I said I couldn't see her. She even wanted us to move in together but I wasn't ready for that. So...'

'So what?'

'I told her we needed a break. I didn't actually break up, but to be honest I don't think I want to get back with her. It was then, and only then, she started going on about being late. I don't believe her. We were careful.'

'Even if you're careful it can still happen. You took advantage of her and then when this happens you ditch her.'

Stu banged his fist down on the table. 'No. It wasn't like that.'

Joe put his hand over Stu's. 'It's okay, mate. Don't yell at Rachel. She's just worried about her pal.'

'Listen, Rachel. It wasn't like what you're saying at all. I needed space so she threw being late in as an extra. If she is pregnant then I'll support the child but I shan't marry her. But I know there isn't one. She's lying. I don't trust her and I don't think she's mentally well. And I don't mean that nastily. Seriously, she needs professional help.'

'You're just saying that to get yourself off the hook.' Though something in me knew he may be telling the truth. Look how she'd reacted with me leaving Woolies, and now not speaking to me. Someone was lying. Was it Stu, or was it Linda? Either way one of them was a bloody good liar.

Stu drank back his drink and slammed the tankard down on the table. 'I'm going to go now, Joe. See you in college tomorrow. And Rachel, I promise you I'm telling you the truth. Linda has issues.' He patted Joe on the back.

'See you tomorrow, mate.' Joe turned to me once Stu was out of sight. 'Are you okay?'

'Yes.' I took a sip of the lager and lime. 'I just don't know who to believe. Stu seems genuine but...'

'Stu's been my best mate since first day at Infants. He's telling the truth. How long have you known Linda?'

'Not that long in comparison. Since I started Woolies as a Saturday girl. So around two and half years, I suppose. But I've never seen her act weird like this. She always seemed level-headed. This is so not like her.'

'Fancy a game of darts to take our minds off things?'

'Yeah, go on then. Be ready to be thrashed.'

The whole team gathered in The Red Lion to celebrate Mel's birthday. Once we were all seated, I leaned over and asked Betty, 'Do they do this for everyone?'

Betty chuckled. 'No, duck. Only for special birthdays. Mel's twenty-one today.'

'Oh, I hadn't realised. I should have bought her a present and a card.'

'No worries, duck. We did a collection and your name went on the card.'

'But I didn't put in any money or sign the card.' I sensed my cheeks burning up.

'Shh. It's okay. You weren't around so I signed for you and we did the collection before you were here. Mel will be none the wiser.'

Mr Strange brought an aluminium ice bucket with a bottle of champagne over to the table and John carried a tray with eight crystal flutes. My boss flipped the cork, and after it popped, poured sparkling wine into each of the glasses. 'Please raise your glasses and join me to congratulate Miss Brown on her twenty-first.'

We all raised our flutes and said, 'Congratulations, Mel.'

'Thank you, everyone.' Mel's face turned almost as red as her hair.

Betty handed her a small parcel wrapped in birthday gift paper. 'This is from us all.'

Mel ripped off the packaging and took out a silver bangle. Her face lit up. 'This is so cool, and you've even had my name engraved. How did you know I've been longing for one of these?'

'Sam may have helped us out there.' Betty's eyes twinkled.

The bartender brought over a selection of sandwiches including cheese and pickle, ham and tomato, and egg and cress. He placed the plates onto the tables.

'Eat up, everyone,' Mr Strange said selecting a cheese and pickle sarnie. I did the same.

It was wonderful getting to know the team as there wasn't much time during working hours. Mary had twin boys who were at Juniors, Lizzie had an elderly mother to care for which is why she only worked mornings. Betty had a grown-up family, two boys and one girl, and Mel was engaged to Sam.

We had an extended lunch break but as the hand on the clock approached two, Mr Strange stood up. 'I think we should be getting back to work. Finish off your food and drinks ladies and gentlemen and follow me over.' He put on his jacket and left the pub.

Everyone got up in turn and I made my way to the office with Mel and Betty. I loved my job and I loved my new friends.

Chapter Twenty

Peggy

Adam cleared the breakfast dishes from the table as I ran the water into the sink, adding a squirt of washing-up liquid.

'What time are you meeting Rachel?' he asked.

'One o'clock.' I lowered the dirty plates into the soapy water. 'It's almost three weeks since I've seen her as, if you remember, she cancelled our last meet-up.'

'So, she doesn't know yet about Mike's letter?' Adam took the tea towel off the hook and dried the dishes as I placed them on the draining board.

'No. She has no idea, only that I have news from him.'

He threw the tea towel across a dining chair and turned me to him. 'And you're going to make it clear that there's no way you're going to the States with her?'

I turned back to the sink. 'I'll encourage her to invite him over here to England first and then it won't be so tough if she visits him later on her own or with a friend.'

'Just make sure you do, Peg. Our Kate needs you at home not galivanting around with an ex-boyfriend.'

'You don't need to remind me of my obligations, Adam. Is this going to be another row? If so, you can bloody finish off the washing-up by yourself.'

'It doesn't have to be an argument. Just remember where your loyalties lie. With me and the kids. Rachel has a mother and father and while I've supported you in getting to know her, I will not let this affect our kids.'

'Fine.' I pulled the plug from the sink and rinsed cold water to remove the soapsuds. 'I'll be home in time to prepare our evening meal. Don't worry, I shall fulfil my obligations.' I stormed out of the kitchen and upstairs to the bathroom to get ready.

<hr/>

I walked into town to save on the bus fare and was glad I did as the scent of the late spring flowers was a delight. One garden I passed was full of colour, boasting sweet peas, snapdragons and carnations while another further up the road was packed with pink, red and yellow roses. Rachel was a nature lover so I'd taken a couple of gardening books out from the library to try and learn more about what the flowers were called.

Yesterday I'd had a call from the temp agency saying that I needed more experience and had I considered going to evening classes. That was no good, I was trying to save money not pay out more. Adam was already accusing me of neglecting my duties as a wife and mother, he'd be livid if I said I was going back to school.

As I reached the clock tower Rachel came running over to me. 'Hiya, Peggy, how are you?' She kissed me on the cheek.

'Fine thank you. I've missed you.'

'Yeah, sorry about that. Been so busy, what with the new job and problems with my best friend. I'll tell you about it over coffee. Unless you'd rather go to the pub?'

'Coffee will be fine.'

We made for the Wimpy bar. I peeped through the window. 'It's a bit busy in there. Looks like everyone's out today. Why don't we go to the park and get a coffee?'

'That's a good idea.'

We sauntered along the footpath and up an alley as a shortcut. The park was looking amazing with the maple trees now turned burnished red. The kiosk was quiet with just a couple of people waiting. Once we had bought the drinks, we made our way to the duck pond and took a seat close to the bank.

'How's the job going?' I asked.

'It's amazing. I really love it. Betty, my supervisor, said I'm picking it up really quickly. Yesterday I answered a couple of phone calls on the switchboard and transferred them without cutting them off.' She beamed.

'You're very lucky to have got the job without experience.' I thought of how I was struggling to even get a position as a filing clerk.

'Yes, I know. Anyway, didn't you say you had some news about Mike?'

'I did.' I passed her the envelope.

She put her coffee cup down on the bench and scanned the letter. 'He said he'll send two tickets over. You will come with me, won't you?'

'No, love, I'm sorry but I can't. It wouldn't be right.'

'But I need you. You have to come. You can't expect me to go over there on my own. Are you going to let me down again?'

'Don't say that, Rachel.'

'Well then. Say you'll come.'

'Why not encourage Mike to come over here and once you've got to know him you could maybe go to the States for a holiday and take Linda or Joe.'

She bit her lip. 'Hmm, I suppose so but I'd rather go with you.'

'It's not a great time for me to leave right now. Kate's not doing so well.'

'What's the matter with her?'

'I'd rather not say.'

She tossed her head. 'I see. I thought I was supposed to be part of your family. When am I going to meet my brother and sister anyway?'

'Soon but now isn't the right time. Apart from the fact I'm enjoying it just being us two for now.'

'If you say so.' She picked up her cup and sulked. Kate would never have done that.

Chapter Twenty-One

Rachel

Jenny barged into my room. 'Do you plan to stay in bed all day?'

I rubbed my eyes. 'Not all day. Why?'

'Mum and Dad have gone out and I'm bored. Wondered if you fancied doing something together. Seems ages since we had sister time. We used to be close before all this adoption business.'

I dragged myself up to a sitting position. 'What are you suggesting?'

'Shopping? Thought you could offer some ideas of what to buy you as it's your birthday next week.'

'I'd love to, Jen,' I answered, 'but I've something planned.'

'Like what?' She flopped down on my bed.

'I'm going to see Linda's mam.'

'Why?'

'Something's not adding up. I thought maybe she'll be able to shed some light on things.'

'Okay.' She pulled the covers off me. 'Get your lazy bod out of bed and we'll go shopping.'

'I just said'– I covered myself back up – 'I'm going to see Linda's mam.'

'And I heard you. Shopping first. Then you go and see Linda Smith's mother while I buy your present. Simple.'

That didn't sound like a bad idea. 'All right but make me a brew and a slice of toast while I get dressed.'

⇜

'That was lovely.' Jenny placed her knife and fork down. 'I've missed our special days out. Haven't you?'

'I have. We should do it more often.' I dropped ten pence tip onto the tray. 'There's nothing quite like sister time and a Wimpy special to cheer us up.' We'd spent the previous hour and half window-shopping for a birthday gift idea for me.

'Can you lend me two pounds?'

'Do you mean I've got to pay for my own pressie?'

'No. I wouldn't do that but there's a new top I've seen in the Chelsea Girl sale. If I wait until I get my monthly allowance from Dad it'll be gone by then.'

'All right.' I took out a couple of notes from my purse. 'Don't forget to pay me back though.' Even though our parents were well off they said we needed to learn the value of money so we couldn't always have what we wanted. I got up from the table. 'I'll meet you at four o'clock in Elmo's for a quick coffee before we catch the bus home.'

⇜

It started to spit as I trekked down the cobbled street of terraced houses. I stopped at number seven and hit the brass knocker. Mrs Smith answered the door in a turban headscarf with the odd curler peeping out, and a ciggie dangling from her mouth.

'Rachel. Hello. What can I do for you?' She squinted. 'Linda's at work.'

'Yes. I know. It was you I've come to see. May I come in?'

126

'Of course.'

I stepped into the living room onto the threadbare carpet.

'Want a cuppa?'

'That would be lovely.'

'Come on through.'

I followed her into the kitchen and took a seat at the table. She popped the kettle onto the gas stove. 'So what was it you wanted to see me about?'

'Linda. I'm worried about her as she won't speak to me.'

Mrs Smith shook her head. 'Let me make this tea and I'll try to explain. In confidence mind. If she thinks I've been talking about her it won't go down well.' Mrs Smith stubbed the cigarette out in the glass ashtray on the worktop.

'Don't worry, I know how to keep a secret.'

The kettle whistled and she added water into the pot. 'Milk and sugar?'

'Yes, please. Just one sugar.'

After sprinkling in a spoon of sugar she gave the cups a stir and handed me a mug. 'There you go, lovey. Let's go and sit down.'

'Thanks.' I followed her back into the living room and took a seat on the settee. Mrs Smith sat down next to me.

'It's nice to see you,' she said. 'It's been a while. So, Linda...' Mrs Smith lifted the mug to her mouth, and took a sip before putting it down on the teak coffee table. 'Where do I start?'

'When did you get back?'

'Back from where?'

'Linda said you'd buzzed off again with your latest boyfriend.'

Mrs Smith shook her head. 'I don't have a boyfriend, dear. In fact I don't remember the last time I did, chance would be a fine thing. And I've not been away anywhere either. This is what she's like. Our Linda has trouble when she feels people have deserted her. This episode started with Stu, and then you leaving Woolies sent her over the top.'

'So, it's my fault?'

'No, not at all. Just explaining how it started. She's never been able to get over the fact that her dad didn't want her when she was born. He's never been in touch. No contact at all. It's left her with this fear of rejection.'

'At least you didn't reject her. You managed to keep her against all odds. My real mother had me adopted.'

'I hadn't realised that. Sorry.' She bit her lip. 'In hindsight maybe Linda would've been better off if I'd had her adopted. Look at you, a good family and a good job.'

'No, you did the right thing. She's lucky you gave up everything to keep her but I still don't understand why she suddenly seems to hate me. And she's told me some other things about her and Stu.'

'That she's pregnant?'

'So it's true?'

'No. A lie I'm afraid. She felt threatened when he didn't want to move in with her.'

'She told you this?'

'Not in those words but she told me she was moving in with him and when it didn't happen...'

'How do you know she's not pregnant?'

'The packet of Dr Whites disappeared as usual from her drawer.'

'I see.'

Mrs Smith took another sip, placed her mug back down, and leaned forward. 'No, I'm not sure you do. She had an episode similar to this at thirteen when her best friend moved away. At thirteen I could get her help, and arranged counselling through the school, but at nineteen I can't do anything about it.' She broke down in tears.

'Mrs Smith, I'm so sorry. Is there anything I can do?'

She patted my hand. 'Just don't give up on your friend.'

'I've an idea. It's my birthday a week on Monday, and obviously that day we'll both be at work, but how about I come around in the afternoon of the Sunday before? Perhaps we can have tea and try and get Linda to open up a bit.'

'I'm not sure she'll agree.'

'Don't tell her I'm coming. Shall we say around two o'clock?'

'I suppose it's worth a try. Thank you for trying.'

'It's the least I can do. She's been a good friend to me up until now.' I glanced at the clock on the wall. Half past three. 'I should go as I'm meeting my sister.' I drank the rest of my drink and placed the cup down on the coffee table. 'Thanks for the tea, Mrs Smith. Let's hope our plan works. Linda means a lot to me.'

As I reached Elmo's I caught sight of Jenny waving from inside.

'How did you get on?' she asked as I took the seat opposite her.

'Good, but I can't talk about it as I promised Mrs Smith.'

'Sounds ominous.'

'Nothing to worry about. Coffee?'

'Yes, thanks. Want to see my new blouse?' Before I could answer she took out a navy spotted crêpe shirt from a paper carrier and held it up against her. It brought out the blue in her eyes.

'I like it.' I leaned across and touched the material.

'Isn't it gorgeous? Oh look, here's the waiter.'

I looked up with shock. 'Joe. I thought you were helping your dad today?'

'They had a crisis here. No one to work. Couldn't say no when I was being offered double time.' He leaned in closer and kissed me on the cheek. 'Fab to see you, babe. What can I get you both?'

'Two coffees please.'

'Aren't you going to introduce us?' Jenny said.

Joe glanced at me too.

'Er, yes of course. Joe this is my sister, Jenny. Jenny this is Joe.'

Joe held out his hand to shake Jenny's. 'Pleased to meet you. You're almost as gorgeous as your sister.'

'So, you're the mystery man. Mum and Dad have been asking Rachel to bring you home for tea. When are you coming?'

'As soon as I get an invite. Two coffees coming up.' He made his way into the kitchen.

'Wow. No wonder you're keeping him to yourself. Scared he might fancy me instead?'

I slapped her hand. 'Don't be stupid. I'd just rather it be him and me for a while.'

'Mum and Dad would approve, I'm sure. You should bring him home.'

Chapter Twenty-Two

Peggy

Adam hovered at the lounge doorway. 'Are you going to fiddle with that letter all day? I presume it's from him. What does he say?'

'He's coming over in two weeks and has asked me to book him a room.'

'Can't he do that himself?' Adam huffed. 'Or perhaps Rachel should do it?'

I put the envelope down on the coffee table. 'Oh, Adam, we're not going to have another row, are we? I don't understand where this jealousy has come from.'

He slumped down onto the settee next to me. 'Can't you? I wonder how you'd feel if it was me meeting up with an ex.'

'But it was so long ago.' I cuddled up to him. 'You know how much I love you. You should trust me.'

'It's not you I have the problem with. It's him. Those yanks have a way of turning a girl's heart.'

I squeezed his hand. 'Well, he's not going to turn mine. Look, Adam, if you're that worried why don't you come with Rachel and me to meet him? I've nothing to hide.'

He brushed his lips against mine. 'You know what, Peg, I may well do that.' He moved away from me. 'There was something else I wanted to speak to you about.'

'Nothing to do with Mike?'

'No, someone far more important. I heard our Kate being sick again last night. You don't think she's…'

I blinked. 'When you say again, how often?'

'The last few days. Do you think she is?'

'No, I don't, but I almost wish she was.'

Adam shot up from the settee. 'What? What kind of stupid thing is that to say about your daughter who's not yet sixteen?'

'Because it would be the lesser of two evils. Sit back down, Adam.'

He perched himself on the edge of the chair. 'I'm waiting.'

'Have you noticed how much weight she's lost?'

'Hmm, now you mention it, yes.'

'And she barely touches her food. And she's always out running, and now with you saying she's being sick. I think she's making herself sick. I think she's got something called anorexia nervosa.'

'What the hell is that?'

'An eating disorder. A friend of Sheila's at school had it.' I covered my mouth. 'Oh my God, Adam. Sheila's friend died. Heart failure, I think. Something to do with complications from the anorexia. What are we going to do? Who should we see?'

'For pity's sake, Peg, why am I only just hearing about this now?'

'It's only been a few weeks and I hoped I was wrong but now with you saying she's being sick, I'm not so sure.'

Adam got up again. 'I'll tell you why, Peg.' His face reddened. 'I'll tell you exactly why. It's because you're too wrapped up with Rachel and Mike. That's the problem. And it's probably the reason why our daughter's resorted to such drastic actions.' He sighed. 'We need to get her to open up.'

'It's nothing to do with me and Rachel, more likely her exams. You know how much she puts herself under pressure to get top marks.'

'No matter what it is. Cancel your plans today so we can get to the bottom of this.'

'No, I can't do that, Rachel's expecting me.'

'Rachel again.'

'Stop it, Adam. You said you supported me in this.'

'Not when it gets in the way of our daughter's health.'

'Kate's out anyway and I'll be back in before she is.'

'And you can forget those mad ideas about getting a job. Our Kate needs you.'

The Towers was packed when I headed in, probably because it was a Sunday. Thank goodness I'd booked a table. Adam had tucked a couple of quid into my purse and told me to enjoy myself. Mind you, that was before the argument. It would've made no difference whether I stayed at home or not as Kate was out with a friend all day. I needed to do something special for Rachel as it was her birthday next week and I was sure she'd be with her family or boyfriend, so no chance of me seeing her then.

'I've a table booked in the name of Davies,' I said to the maître d'.

He put on his glasses to check the appointment diary. 'Ah, yes, here you are. Table for two at one o'clock. Come this way.' He led me to a small round table at the back of the restaurant. 'Would madam care for a drink while waiting for your guest?'

'No, thank you. I'll wait. She should be here any moment.' I looked up towards the entrance. 'Here she is now.' I waved and

Rachel wandered over. The head waiter pulled back the chair for her to sit down.

'Thank you.' Her brown eyes sparkled.

He placed a menu in front of each of us. 'I'll give you a few minutes to get settled.'

'How have you been?' I asked Rachel.

'Good thanks. The job's amazing and I've made some new friends. It was Mel's birthday on Thursday, she's secretary to the journalist. Well because it was her birthday, we all went over to the pub at lunchtime and I found out lots more about them all. Mel's engaged to Sam, the photographer. Mel wants to meet up with me and Joe, a week tomorrow, as it's the day before my birthday.'

'That's why I booked here today. I imagined you'd be busy next week with either your parents or boyfriend. I've got...'

The waitress interrupted me. 'Are you ready to order?' Her dark uniform with a frilly white apron and small hat took me back all those years ago when I was in London waitressing and where I met Adam. Adam my lovely, kind, sensitive Adam. Not the jealous Adam who'd appeared in our house the last few weeks.

'What do you recommend?' I asked.

'The sole's on special, madam, and delicious I'm told.'

'Do you fancy the fish?' I asked Rachel.

'Yes, all right.'

'Would madams like it with fries or potatoes and veg?'

'Fries for me, please.' Rachel grinned.

'I'll have the same.'

'And drinks?'

'Do you like Riesling?' I asked Rachel. 'It would be nice to have a glass of wine to celebrate your birthday.'

'Not sure, I've never tried it. Happy to try though.'

I looked up at the waitress. 'A bottle of Riesling then, please.' I passed my unopened menu to her and Rachel did the same.

'I won't be long.' The young, blonde-haired woman hurried away from our table.

'As I was saying' – I took the small package from my bag – 'here's a little present from Adam and me.'

'Oh, thank you, Peggy. Can I open it now?'

'Please do.' I watched with anticipation as she ripped off the wrapping and opened the small box revealing a pair of cubic zirconia stud earrings.

'I love them. Thank you.'

A waiter brought over the bottle of wine and poured a drop into my glass. 'Would madam care to try?'

'Yes, thank you.' I tasted the wine. 'Mmm, yes, that's lovely.'

He filled our glasses and dropped the bottle into an ice bucket on the table. 'Your meals will be with you shortly.'

'Please could we have a jug of water and two glasses?' I asked.

'Certainly, madam.' He left our table and stopped to speak to a young waiter.

Rachel sipped the wine.

'Do you like it?'

'It's slightly sweet, but good. I think I like it.' She giggled.

'It's my favourite,' I said as the waitress arrived with our meal and put a plate in front of each of us. 'I've heard from Mike,' I said, squeezing the slice of lemon onto my fish.

'You have?'

'Yes. He's coming over at the end of the month and has asked me to book him into a hotel. I thought perhaps The George. What do you think?'

'Sure. You'll be meeting him with me, won't you?'

The young waiter who looked younger than Neil brought across a jug of water and two glasses to the table. 'Would you like me to pour?' he asked.

'No, it's fine, thank you.' I smiled.

'Very well.' He turned away and made for another table.

'Well?' Rachel poured out a glass of water for each of us.

'Sorry?'

'You will be meeting him with me?'

Would I? If Adam had his way I wouldn't and what of Kate? What if she were seriously ill? I brushed those thoughts away. 'Yes, of course. Adam may join us too.'

'What date does Mike arrive?'

'29th June. So not too long for you to wait.'

She grinned. 'How long's he over for?'

'He didn't say but I imagine at least a couple of weeks.'

'I'll have to work on the weekdays as it's not enough notice for me to ask for time off but that still leaves evenings and weekends. Maybe we could go into Chester one Saturday. I'm sure he'd love to see the sights.'

'I imagine he'd like that. It'll bring back some memories I'm sure.'

Chapter Twenty-Three

Rachel

The sun was already hot and it wasn't yet eleven. I rummaged through my wardrobe and selected my new pink gingham smock dress. Its puffed sleeves were all the rage. I'd wear it with my white sandals.

'Morning, Mum,' I said on entering the kitchen.

'You're up at last.'

'What do you mean?'

'We've all been to early morning Holy Communion. I had hoped you'd join us.'

'Sorry. I was too tired.'

Mum shook her head. 'Perhaps you wouldn't be too tired if you hadn't stayed out so late last night.'

'Maybe not.' I didn't want a row. Things had been a lot better since I'd started working at the newspaper. 'What are you making?'

Mum smiled and tapped her nose.

'Is it a cake for me?'

'Mind your own, young lady. You'd better get yourself something to eat.'

I popped a couple of Mother's Pride slices of bread into the toaster and flicked the electric kettle. 'Tea, Mum?'

'No thank you. What are your plans today?'

'I'm meeting a friend shortly and this evening I'm seeing Joe. Mel and Sam from work are joining us for a meal.'

'Joe, he's the boyfriend?' She spooned the mixture into two sandwich tins and put them in the oven.

'Yes.'

'So, when are we going to meet him?'

'Probably soon. Jenny met him when we were out last week. She liked him.'

'Well don't leave it too long. It would be nice to meet the young man our daughter is dating.'

'To check him over you mean?'

'No. It's called showing an interest.' She untied her full-length pinny and hung it on the door hook. 'And who's this friend you're seeing this afternoon? Not Peggy again, is it?'

'No. I saw her last week. She gave me a pair of studded earrings for my birthday.' I took the golden slices from the toaster.

'Who then?'

'Just a friend from work,' I lied.

'Okay, enjoy yourself. I need to hang out the washing.' She picked up the laundry basket.

'I'm surprised you don't have the cleaning woman do the laundry.'

Mum tutted. 'Just because we have money, Rachel, doesn't mean we can squander it. Twice a week is enough for someone to come in and help with the house. Godly hands don't stay idle.' She unlocked the back door and trudged out to the garden.

It was dead on two o'clock when I knocked on number seven and Mrs Smith opened the door. Bouncy, dark waves framed her oval face and without the normal ciggie dangling from her mouth she looked really attractive. She could easily find a man. I wondered why she hadn't.

'Hello there, Rachel,' she said raising her voice, 'what a lovely surprise. It's been a long time since we've seen you around here. Linda will be pleased.'

As I entered the sitting room Linda shot up from the couch and made for the stairs.

'Please don't go, Lind.'

'Give the girl a chance,' Mrs Smith said. 'Just hear her out.'

Linda grunted flopping back down and folding her arms. 'You've got five minutes.'

'You'll stay for tea, Rachel? I've made a Victoria sponge.'

'Yes, please, Mrs Smith. Thank you.'

I took a seat next to my friend and touched her hand. 'I've missed you. Please talk to me.'

'What's there to say? You've got your new job, your new fiancé, and your new mother. What have I got?'

'You've got your lovely mam, your supervisor's job at Woolies which you love, and you've got me as your mate if you'll still have me.' I caught a glimpse of a smile but it didn't last long.

'I'm not in the mood for talking.'

'All right we can play cards or something. I've got time.'

With a glint in her eyes, she rose from the couch, headed over to the sideboard drawer and pulled out a pack of cards. 'Mam, we're going to play Pontoon,' she said, 'want to join us?'

'That'll be nice. We haven't played for a long time.'

Linda made for the kitchen. 'Come on,' she said to me and Mrs Smith. We followed and I joined her at the table.

'I'll be banker.' She grinned. 'Mam, grab some matches for bets.'

Mrs Smith took a box of Swan Vesta from the shelf. She gave me a nodding smile and sat down opposite. Our plan was working. I knew Linda wouldn't be able to resist a game.

She dealt two cards to each of us. 'Twist or stick?'

I looked at my cards. A queen of hearts and six of diamonds 'Twist.'

She turned over a jack of spades.

'Bust.' I laid my cards down.

'Mam?'

'Stick.'

Linda flipped her hand revealing an ace of clubs and king of spades. 'Pontoon. I win.' She raked in the matchsticks.

We continued playing over the next hour, only stopping to drink tea and eat some of Mrs Smith's delicious moist cake.

Once Linda had won all the matches, I broached the subject. 'It's my birthday tomorrow.'

'I do know.' She shuffled the deck before putting it back into the box. 'Just because we've not seen each other doesn't mean I've had a memory lapse. You doing anything special?'

'Working in the day and seeing Joe in the evening.'

'How is the new job?'

'Cool. I love it but miss seeing you every day.'

'Really?'

'Of course.'

'More tea, girls?' Mrs Smith poured tea into our cups without waiting for an answer.

'Thanks.' I took a sip.

'Have you seen Stu?' Linda's eyes filled.

'A couple of times. Are you really pregnant?'

She shook her head. 'No. I wish I was though. At least then he'd have to marry me.'

'You can't make someone marry you.'

'He'd have to if I were up the duff.'

'No, he wouldn't.' I got up from the chair and put my arm around her. 'Don't waste your life, Lind. You're gorgeous. Someone out there will love you for who you are.'

'All right for you to say when you've got everything.'

'You've got your mam,' I repeated. 'A mam who gave up everything to keep you. Listen' – I pulled a chair close and sat back down – 'don't get cross but your mam said you got upset like this a few years back.'

Linda scowled at Mrs Smith.

'Don't blame her. I made her speak to me. But she said you had some kind of counselling last time and it helped.'

'So.'

'Maybe it could help again?'

'I'm not sure. I was a kid then and it was easier to talk about stuff.'

I squeezed her fingers. 'Worth a try though, surely?'

She closed her eyes for a second. 'I'll think about it.'

'That's all we ask.' I picked up my cup and drank the rest of my tea. 'I'll see you next week? Perhaps we could meet Wednesday lunchtime and arrange an evening to go out and celebrate our birthdays, as we missed yours last month.'

'All right. I'll see you outside the shop at one.'

I glanced up at Mrs Smith who looked so pretty when she smiled.

Chapter Twenty-Four

Rachel

Sam took over the ordering as he was used to eating in an Indian restaurant.

'Four poppadoms and chutney accompaniments, one chicken madras, one prawn balti, one chicken korma, one lamb vindaloo, two pilau and two special fried rice. And to share we'll have a Bombay aloo, saag aloo, mushroom bhaji. Oh, and bhindi bhaji, ladies' fingers.' He looked across at us. 'Breads?'

Mel answered, 'Yes let's have two naans and two chapati.'

The waiter wrote everything down. 'Drinks?'

'One pint of bitter, a lemonade, and two cokes, as it seems I'm the only one drinking.' Sam closed the menu. 'I think that's everything.'

Joe and I nodded. We were excited to try Indian cuisine.

'So, it's your birthday tomorrow then?' Sam asked.

'Yes.'

The waiter placed our drinks down in front of us.

'Thank you.' I smiled at him.

Sam took a gulp from his pint. 'And how old will you be?'

'Nineteen. How old are you?'

'Twenty-five next month.'

The waiter returned but this time with poppadoms and chutneys. 'Your meal will be ready shortly,' he said before heading over to a large party who'd just arrived.

Mel helped herself to a poppadom from the silver platter and scooped a teaspoon of mango chutney onto her plate.

Joe and I did the same.

'We're both Geminis,' Mel said to me. 'How about you, Joe? When's your birthday?' She nibbled on the poppadom.

'22nd October. Mmm. This is good.'

'Ooh that makes you a Libra but only just as you're on the cusp. Sam's a Leo. I love horoscopes, don't you Rachel?'

'To be honest I don't know anything about them.' I spooned mango chutney onto my poppadom.

'Christ, Mel, don't start that horoscope rubbish again.' Sam downed the rest of his drink. He sighed. 'You bloody bring this up every time we're out with someone new.'

Mel blushed. If Joe had spoken to me like that, I'd have swiped him one. 'How long have you two been engaged?' I asked, trying to calm the situation.

'We got engaged last year on my birthday,' Mel answered. 'And we're planning to get married next year, aren't we, Sam?'

'Indeed. Where's that food? I'm starving.' He waved to the waiter.

The waiter rushed over. 'Yes, sir?'

'How long's our food going to take? And can you get me another pint of bitter?'

'Yes, sir.' The waiter hurried off.

'I didn't think we'd been waiting that long,' I said.

'Little girl, you obviously have no idea how restaurants work.'

My pulse pounded. 'I'm not a little girl and I've been in plenty of restaurants, thank you.'

The waiter returned with Sam's drink. 'Your food's almost ready.'

'Thank you,' I said as Sam didn't.

Joe bit into a poppadom. 'We're engaged.'

'Oh really?' Mel looked at my hand. 'No ring?'

'I do have a ring but as we haven't told my parents yet I don't wear it on my finger. Normally it's on a chain around my neck but difficult with this top.'

'We have so much in common, Rachel.' Mel beamed. 'Have you set a date yet?'

I didn't think we had a lot in common at all. Just because we were both engaged and had the same star sign. 'Not yet,' I answered. 'Ooh look, here comes our dinner.'

The waiter pulled a trolley up to our table and placed some food warmers down. He looked at Sam. 'Sorry for the delay, sir. Chicken madras?'

Joe put up his hand and the waiter placed the dish by the side of him. The balti was arranged close to Mel, the vindaloo next to Sam, and the korma by me, with the sides and rice dishes positioned on the warmers.

I spooned out a helping of the curry, added a bit of everything else and took a taste. 'Mmm. It's lovely. Wait till I tell my sister I've been to an Indian. She'll be envious.'

'You must feel like the odd man out, Joe,' Sam said, 'what with us all working at the newspaper. What do you do?'

'I'm still at college but training to be a motor mechanic. I love getting my hands dirty.'

'College? For God's sake, pal, how old are you?' Sam tucked into his vindaloo.

Joe's face paled. 'Eighteen this October.'

'Bloody hell. Barely out of nappies,' Sam answered with a mouthful of food.

I was seething. Should I say something? Would that make it worse for Joe? I glanced at him for guidance. He nodded as if to say it's okay but it wasn't okay. I took a deep breath and said, 'Better than being an old timer, I suppose,' and laughed.

Mel and Joe joined in with the laughter. Sam sniggered. 'You got me there, Rachel. I can see we're going to have to watch you.'

'Oi' – Mel elbowed Sam – 'behave. Take no notice of him,' she said to me, 'you'll get used to his weird sense of humour.'

I rolled my eyes. 'You mean he's like this all the time?'

'I'm afraid so. See what I have to put up with.' Mel's comment seemed to have put Sam in his place for a while as his tone changed and he asked, 'How are you enjoying your meal?'

'It's very nice. Thanks for suggesting it.' I was wishing we were here with Stu and Linda though. I hadn't seen this side of Sam at work but then I hadn't had a lot to do with him. He was really starting to wind me up.

'How do you get on with the future in-laws?' Sam asked Joe.

Joe chuckled. 'I'll find out tomorrow. Rachel's finally agreed to me meeting them. Her mam's doing a special birthday tea.'

Mel tapped Joe's arm. 'I'm sure you've got nothing to worry about. Sam loves my mum and dad. Sam's parents live in Germany so I've yet to meet them, but we're hoping to get over there later this year.'

Sam may love Mel's parents but I wondered what they thought of him. Fancy having someone like him for a future son-in-law.

'So, Rachel' – Sam chewed a chunk of naan – 'you're a bit of a cradle-snatcher, then?'

I sensed myself blushing. 'Not by much.' I pretended to laugh.

'Joe obviously likes the older woman' – Sam winked – 'hey Joe?'

Mel prodded him. 'Shut up, Sam. Leave them alone. They won't want to come out with us again.'

'I'm only making conversation.' Sam dipped the naan into his curry. 'So which party do you vote for? Oh no, that's right, you're not old enough to vote.' He roared with laughter.

Joe gripped his fists but looked at me and smiled before glaring at Sam. 'No, that's correct. I've got that pleasure to come.'

We continued to eat while Sam made me feel out of my depth chatting politics. I reckoned he was trying to intimidate us. Mel mouthed I'm sorry. The evening was a disaster. This was certainly the last time we'd be going out with them. I really missed going out with Linda and Stu. I wondered if she agreed to counselling and got better whether she and Stu might get back together.

Joe took a sip of his drink. 'So, what motor do you drive, Sam?'

He slurred his words. 'I don't drive.'

'You've passed your test though?' Joe pushed.

'Er, no. Driving's never interested me.'

'That must be tricky getting around on your assignments,' I said.

'Not really. The newspaper just orders a car for me.'

The waiter cleared the dishes from the table and left a dessert menu.

Mel picked the card up. 'Yum, pudding.' She grinned.

Joe raised his eyebrows. 'So how did you two manage to get here this evening? Taxi?'

'No,' Mel answered, 'I'm the driver.'

'Crikes, I'd hate a woman driving me around.' Joe squeezed my hand. 'I either have the use of Dad's car or my bike. Ever been on a motorbike, Sam?'

'Can't say I have, pal.'

Good for Joe putting Sam in his place but it was now turning into male rivalry. I checked the time on my watch. 'I think we should be making a move. Do you mind, Mel?'

She shifted her gaze around the room. 'No, of course not.'

'I'll get the bill.' Sam put his hand up to alert the waiter and mimed bill.

In no time at all the waiter brought across the tab along with hot flannels for us to freshen up, and small sweets to suck. Joe got out his wallet but Sam said, 'No, this is my treat. A birthday present for Rachel from me and Mel.'

Mel glimpsed at me and smiled.

'You're okay, mate.' Joe dropped a couple of pound notes on the silver tray. 'That should cover our share.' He turned to me. 'Ready?'

⚓

The following afternoon, Joe pulled up outside my house. I rushed to the front door and opened it as he stepped out of the 1600E and waved. Looking handsome in a light blue Brutus shirt and Levi jeans, he hurried up the footpath. His hair was neatly tied back in a ponytail.

'Wow. You look smart.' I kissed him briefly on the lips.

'And you look gorgeous.' He squeezed my hand. 'Lamb to the slaughter then. Best get on with it. Let's hope it goes better than last night.'

'Yes, that was awful. Sorry about that. I'd no idea Sam could be so obnoxious. I reckon he'd been drinking before they turned up. Mum and Dad are nothing like him. It will be fine.'

'Hope so.' His hand trembled in mine.

'Come on.' We strode down the hallway and into the dining room. 'Dad,' I said, 'this is Joe.'

'How do you do, Joe?' Dad shook Joe's hand. 'It's good to finally meet you. I hope you're hungry. Mrs Webster likes to put on a feast whenever we have visitors.'

'How do you do, sir.' Joe dropped his hand. 'Yes, I'm...' he stopped himself. 'That sounds wonderful.'

Mum had gone all out with the setting of the round table. She'd dressed it in a white Egyptian linen cloth with matching napkins. A silver candelabra holding three candles stood in the centre, with a crystal glass tumbler set at each named place with our best silver-plated cutlery.

Jenny charged into the room, made straight for Joe, and planted a kiss on the side of his cheek. 'You managed to convince her then? It's good to see you again. Mum's made a roast.'

Before he had a chance to answer, Mum entered the room with a huge joint of beef on an oval platter.

'Mum,' I said, 'meet Joe.'

She put the meat down on the table and shook Joe's hand. 'Happy to finally meet you, young man. Do sit down. Rachel, show Joe where to sit.'

Dad took a seat on the beech carver and pulled the beef platter in front of him. I checked the name place cards, and pulled out a chair adjacent to Dad. 'I'm here, Joe, and you're next to me.' That left Jenny in the middle of Joe and Mum, and Dad the other side of her.

'Jennifer, can you help me bring in the food please?' Mum tucked loose strands of blonde hair behind her ear.

I went to get up.

'No, it's all right, Rachel,' she said, 'you stay and entertain your guest.'

Mum and Jenny carried in serving dishes laden with roast potatoes, sprouts, carrots and peas, a jug of gravy, and a plate of massive Yorkshire puddings. Once Mum and Jenny had taken their seats, Dad began carving the meat and passed around the plates in turn. Joe glanced at me wide-eyed.

With our plates stacked with food, Dad began the interrogation. 'So, Joe, what is it you do?'

'I'm still at college studying motor mechanics.'

'You like playing around with cars?'

'Yes, I've been tinkering with engines almost since I could walk. My father's in the motor trade. He's a foreman at the British Leyland garage.'

'Yet you drive a Ford.'

'Yes. It's Dad's. He allows me to use it. We used to have a Triumph but my m... mum wanted the 1600E.' Joe shrugged. 'So he did a part exchange. Anything to keep my mum happy.'

Dad picked up the bottle of red. 'Wine, Joe?'

'No thank you. I never drink when driving, particularly in my dad's baby.'

Dad looked at Mum and they gave each other a nod of approval.

Chapter Twenty-Five

Peggy

Adam folded up the newspaper. 'We need to tackle her now?'

'I'm not so sure. That could make her even more sneaky if she thinks we're on to her?'

'Well, I'm not sitting here doing bloody nowt.' He got up from the dining chair, moved towards the door, and shouted upstairs, 'Kate, downstairs now.'

'Why?' she called down.

'It's dinner time.'

'I'm not hungry.'

'I don't give a damn whether you're hungry or not, get down here now or I'll come and drag you down.'

I hurried over next to him. 'Adam, don't.' I tugged at his arm.

He shoved me away. 'You might be happy to let our daughter starve herself but I'm not. Kate,' he yelled, 'are you coming or am I coming to get you?'

'I'm coming.' Kate sloped downstairs and followed us into the kitchen. She took a seat at the table. 'Honestly, Dad, I'm not hungry. I had a huge meal at college.'

Adam and I sat back down. 'Now why don't I believe you?' he said. 'Look your mother's made chicken chasseur. Your favourite.'

I glared at Adam and he glared back at me. 'Come on, Kate,' his voice softened, 'just a few forkfuls for your old dad.' He smiled.

'I'll try.' Kate picked up her cutlery and scooped a forkful into her mouth.

'That's a good girl,' Adam coaxed, 'and another one.'

'Dad, please don't make me. I'm full.'

'Just a few more, darling. It's only cos we love you.'

After half a dozen forkfuls she set her cutlery down. 'No more, Dad.'

Adam patted the back of her hand. 'All right, Kate, but tomorrow you must eat breakfast. I'm going to watch you like a hawk from now on until I see you start eating properly again.'

She closed her eyes momentarily. 'Can I go now?'

Adam nodded, sat back in the chair and continued to eat his meal.

'You know she's probably in the bathroom now throwing up?'

'Well at least I'm trying. What are you bloody doing? Off out to meet your fancy man and adopted daughter.'

'Aren't you coming with me tomorrow?'

'How can I? One of us has to stay with Kate. You could always cancel and spend the afternoon with your family instead of gadding about.'

I put my hand on his but he pulled it back. 'It's not like that. You know it's not. You said you supported me in getting to know Rachel.'

'Getting to know Rachel, yes, not getting to know your bloody ex all over again.' He slammed down his cutlery. 'I've had enough.' He shoved his plate away.

Adam strode in from work just before one. I'd set out quiche and salad on the table ready. Normally when he came in, I'd get a kiss but not today. Instead, he pushed past me and said, 'I'm going up to get changed,' and stomped upstairs. I heard him knock on Kate's door. Her door opened and closed.

There was nothing I could do, I had to go today. I'd promised Rachel that I would meet Mike with her. How could I let her down again? Mike was here for Rachel not me.

Kate's door opened and closed again, and Adam stomped across the landing. After a few minutes he came downstairs dressed in a blue checked shirt and denim jeans.

'Adam.' I put my arm around him.

He pushed me off. 'Don't.'

'But, Adam, why are you being like this with me? I miss us.'

'Stop thinking about yourself, Peg. Think about our lovely girl wasting away and you not doing a damn thing about it because you're far too busy with your precious Rachel and Mike.'

'That's not true and you know it. I'm always here for my family. Dinner's always on the table whenever you all get in, your clothes are washed and ironed, the house is immaculate. You can't say things like that to me. Don't take it out on me.' I picked up my handbag. 'Lunch is on the table. Oh, and just so you know, I managed to get Kate to eat a bit of grapefruit for breakfast. She loves quiche so hopefully you'll be able to tempt her... but for Christ's sake, don't be so hard on the girl.'

'How dare you?' He charged over to me.

'What? You going to hit me?'

He dropped his hand. 'No, of course not. I'm sorry.'

Soft footsteps came downstairs. 'She's coming,' I said, 'shh.'

'You off out, Mam?'

'Just for a couple of hours, darling. I'll be back in time for dinner. Sit down with Dad and have some lunch. It's your favourite. Neil should be home shortly.' I kissed Kate on the cheek and moved over to Adam and kissed him too. 'I shan't be too long.'

'We'll see you later,' he said.

Torn between Rachel and Kate, I told myself I wouldn't be long. Kate had Adam. Rachel needed me. She'd been taken away from me when she was born which I had no power over but I could be there for her now.

We'd arranged to meet at the clock tower and go to The George together. It was just before two o'clock when I arrived and spotted her coming across the road from the bus stop. I waved and she waved back.

'Hello, Peggy.' She kissed me on the cheek.

'It's good to see you,' I said. 'You look pretty.' She was wearing a pink floral smock with puffed sleeves. 'I love your dress.'

'Thanks. It's new. Bought it last week when I got paid. Needed to look my best to meet Mike. I'm really nervous. I wonder what he's like.'

'I'm nervous too,' I confessed. 'He's going to love you. How could he not?' My heart felt like it was jumping out of my chest it was beating so fast. I was nervous about seeing Mike. Nervous about leaving Kate. And nervous what all this was doing to my once happy marriage that was now in shreds. 'Let's go in.' I hooked my arm in Rachel's. 'Let's meet your father.'

As we strolled through the entrance, I caught sight of him. There could be no doubt. Tawny brown hair flicked across his forehead just like all those years ago. Apart from looking older he was the same. On recognising me, he smiled. The same smile I remembered from when we were together. A casual navy jacket and brown slacks replaced the steel blue uniform. His grin widened and his teeth gleamed. 'Peg. It's good to see you, sweetheart. You've not changed a bit.' He took me in his arms just like he'd done all those years ago. I felt safe and wanted to stay but knew it was wrong so backed away.

'You've not changed either. This is Rachel, your daughter.'

'Rachel, honey' – he hugged her tightly – 'I can't believe I have a daughter. I'd no idea and what a beauty too. I bet you've got all the guys running after you.'

Rachel released herself from his hold and laughed. 'Just the one.'

'Come,' he said, and put an arm around each of us. 'I've booked a table for lunch in the restaurant.'

Over lunch Mike chatted and Rachel held on to his every word. 'Do you have any other children?' she asked him.

'No, honey, you're the only one which is why it was such a wonderful surprise when Peg wrote to me about you. And when I look at you it's like stepping back all those years and being with your mother. You're the image of her.'

Rachel chuckled. 'That's what Adam said.'

'Adam?'

'Adam's my husband. Remember I mentioned him in the letter. Unfortunately, he couldn't be here today as our daughter, Kate, is having a bit of a rough time lately.'

'Nothing serious I hope?'

Rachel's attention was on me as I answered, 'No. Nothing serious but we didn't want to leave her on her own.'

After we'd finished a luncheon of fish and chips, washed down with a glass of shandy, Mike answered all of Rachel's questions with ease. Was he married? He had been but was now divorced. Did he have a girlfriend? He was free and single, he told her, making a point of winking at me. No wonder Adam was jealous with the attention Mike was throwing at me but Adam need not have worried. Seeing Mike at first had made my heart race but afterwards I found I was wishing it was Adam sitting here with us. Mike was too cocky by half.

I glanced at my watch. 'I'm really sorry, Rachel, I must get back to Kate but you should stay and get to know Mike.'

She glared at me with pleading eyes.

'You'll be fine.' I kissed her on the cheek.

'Of course, she will,' Mike said. 'We can go for a stroll if you like, Rachel?'

'Yes, that'll be nice.' Rachel turned to me. 'You're right, Peggy, I'll be fine. I'll give you a ring tomorrow.'

Mike rose from the chair and hugged me. I kissed him on the cheek. 'Enjoy your visit. Rachel will be a good tour guide, I'm sure and no doubt I'll see you again before you leave.'

I left the hotel and hurried home.

Chapter Twenty-Six

Rachel

Mel and I wandered around Maple Park admiring the gorgeous dark green leaves on the trees. On reaching the café kiosk I took loose change from my purse and spoke to the grey-haired man behind the counter, 'A black coffee, please.' I turned to Mel.

'I'll have a tea.' She went to open her handbag.

'No,' I said, 'it's on me.'

The seller's eyes glinted behind his round glasses. 'Anything else?'

'No thanks.' I passed over the exact money.

He poured coffee into one paper cup, and tea into another, and pushed them towards us. 'Have a good day, girls.'

'Cheers.' I picked up the drinks and passed one to Mel. 'Here you go.'

'Thanks.' She slipped her bag over her left shoulder and took the cup. 'Mmm, I needed that. What do you want to do?'

'Let's head for the ducks.' We made for my favourite bench by the pond where half a dozen large goldfish were swimming at the surface around pink and white lilies. 'Wonder where all the geese and ducks are?' I eased down on the wooden seat and Mel sat next to me.

'No idea. Maybe they'll turn up later,' she said. 'Anyway, thanks for coming to lunch with me. I wanted to explain about

Sam's behaviour that night. Sorry I'm only just apologising now but he whisked me off on a surprise holiday to Blackpool. Sorted it out with Mr Strange and everything. Even got my mum to pack a few bits and I had no idea until he turned up at my house early Monday morning in a taxi.'

'So, you thought you were going to work as normal?'

'Yep.'

'I thought it was weird you hadn't mentioned anything.'

'I know. It was such a surprise.'

'Must've been.' I took the cheese and pickle sandwich, which was cut into two triangles, from the Tupperware container. It made me think how Linda and I had always shared our lunches. 'What have you got?' I asked Mel.

'Ham and tomato.'

'Want to share? Mine's cheese and pickle. We could have one of each?'

'No, ta. I don't like cheese.'

'Oh. Okay. So, what gives with Sam? I don't know how you put up with him.' I took a bite of the brown bread.

'He's not normally that bad. I mean booking a surprise holiday for me. He can be so thoughtful, but unfortunately, we'd had a massive row before we met up with you and Joe. Joe seems nice.'

Two mallard and a drake waddled towards us. 'Ah there they are.' I broke the crusts from my sarnie into small pieces and threw the bits towards them. 'Hello, quack quacks,' I said as they charged for the crumbs. 'Look at them.' I chuckled. 'Yes, Joe's lovely. What was your row about?'

'Erm...'

'You don't have to tell me if you'd rather not.'

'Promise not to let on that I told you then?'

'I promise.' I started on my second sandwich.

'He didn't like my nail polish. Said it made me look like a tart.'

'What? You're joking.'

'He doesn't like nail varnish full stop but me wearing the bold blue really pushed him.'

'I wouldn't let any man tell me what I can do.'

'I should never have worn it. I knew he'd be cross, but my sister bought me it for my birthday, and insisted on painting my nails.'

'I thought they looked rather cool. I have a sister too. How old's yours?'

'Twenty-three. I'm always admiring her nail polishes so she bought me a lovely selection.'

'You should get rid of Sam, Mel. He's a nasty piece of work in my book.' I fastened the empty Tupperware container, wishing I had something else to eat. 'He was horrible in the restaurant. If he's like that now imagine what he'll be like once you're married. He'll be controlling everything. Who you can see, what you can wear, even what you can watch on TV. I've heard about men like him.'

'No, you're wrong. He loves me and I love him.'

'I'm a good judge of character and everything about him tells me he's bad news. Joe thought so too.' I glanced at my watch. 'We should get back to work but I'm still starving.'

'That's because you gave half of your sandwich to the ducks.'

'Yeah, I suppose so. I really fancy a Mars but I don't have time to pop into the shop.'

'How come? We've another ten minutes yet.'

'Nah, Lizzie needs relieving from reception as she wants to leave a little earlier.'

'I don't mind going to the shop for you,' she said as we both rose from the bench.

'You sure?' I went to get my purse but she touched my hand and said, 'No. It's my treat. You bought the drinks.'

'Cheers.' Although I was unsure how I'd manage to eat a chocolate bar while on the front of house desk.

'Are you still enjoying the job?' she asked as we wandered out of the park.

'I love it. The only thing I miss is seeing my friend from Woolies. We try and meet up if she has the same lunchtime, but otherwise, I keep Wednesdays free as she has a half day.'

'Did you have a good birthday?'

'Yes. And Joe got on well with my parents. Mum and Dad approved. I think the fact that he made a point of not drinking and driving put him in their good books.' As we reached the gates to the exit, I checked my watch again. 'Gosh. I'd best run. I'll catch you back at work. Thanks for grabbing the Mars.'

⁎

Mike was standing outside The George. 'Peg not with you?' He kissed me on the cheek.

'No, she couldn't make it.'

'Oh, that's a shame. I booked a table for the three of us. I thought we'd celebrate your belated birthday as I missed the actual day, and the last eighteen before.' He took my arm and led me down the corridor to the hotel's restaurant. 'So how was your birthday?'

'Good thanks. My boyfriend met my parents for the first time and they liked him.'

On reaching the entrance he said to the Maître d', 'I've a table booked in the name of Millar.'

'This way, sir.' The host led us to a table decorated with blue and yellow balloons. Mike pulled out a chair for me.

'This is all a bit embarrassing.' I chuckled, feeling myself burning up as I took a seat.

'It was Peg's idea. I can't believe she's backed out. I had to go to great lengths to get us this table on a Friday night.'

I scanned the menu. 'Does it really matter?'

'Quite frankly, yes.'

'Did you come over to England to get to know me or to rekindle your relationship with Peggy?'

'Well, both. Peg and I had something special, and if it hadn't been for her father, it would be me married to her, and you'd have grown up with loving parents.'

I glared at him. 'For your information, I did grow up with loving parents. My mum and dad are the best and I've never wanted for anything. You know I'm beginning to wonder whether you're interested in me at all.' I shot up from the chair.

'Don't be like that. Of course, I want to get to know you. You're my daughter and the only kid I have.' He reached for my hand. 'Please, sit back down and choose whatever you'd like from the menu. We'll have champagne too. Money's no object. Anyhow, you can't go yet because I've bought you a gift.' He dug into his pocket and handed me a small parcel wrapped in gold-coloured paper.

I slumped back down to the chair and ripped off the packaging revealing a blue box. I opened it. 'Earrings. Thanks.'

'The pearls are real. None of the cheap stuff. I noticed you had little rose studs in the other day.'

'Yes, they were from Joe.'

'It would be nice to meet him. Has Peg met him yet?'

'No. He doesn't know I'm adopted and for now I'd like to keep it that way.'

'That's a shame as I really would've liked the chance to meet him and you know I'm only here for another few days.'

'And here to get to know me. Not my boyfriend and not to start up a romance with Peggy.'

'I thought we could go to Chester Zoo tomorrow as you have the day off. Maybe you could bring Joe, and persuade Peg to come. We could have a double date.'

I dropped the menu. 'You know what, Mike. I'm not sure this is going to work.' I got up again. 'Let me know when I become more important to you than Peggy.'

He leapt from his chair and chased after me. 'Don't go, Rachel.'

'You've spoilt it. I'm too angry right now and need time to cool off.'

'You'll come tomorrow though? And bring Peg? We'll get a cab. Meet me here at eleven.'

'I'll think about it.'

Mrs Smith opened the door. 'Hello, Rachel. Linda never mentioned you were coming around this evening. Come in.'

'I hadn't planned to.' I burst into tears.

'Oh dear, what is it?'

'Is she in?'

'Yes, she's up in her room. Go up. Have you eaten?'

'No. My dinner date went a bit pear-shaped.'

'You're welcome to join us. It's just liver and onion casserole.'

'Thanks, I'd like that.' I ventured upstairs and knocked on Linda's door. 'Lind, it's me.'

She opened the door in a pink Crimplene housecoat puffing on a Woodbine. 'This is a nice surprise, but what's up? Looks like you've been crying.'

I flopped on her bed and sobbed again. 'I just can't believe it.'

'What's happened? Not you and Joe, is it?'

'No.' I sniffed, wiping my nose with the back of my hand. 'It's him. Mike. My supposed father. I thought he'd come all this way to get to know me but he's more interested in rekindling his relationship with Peggy.' I pulled a hanky from my sleeve and blew my nose. 'I left him in the restaurant before we'd even had time to order. I was so cross.'

'I don't blame you. I think I'd have been telling him to eff off.'

'I felt like it, I can tell you.' I sighed. 'He wants me to go to Chester Zoo with him tomorrow. Peggy too of course although to be honest I'm not sure she'll make it. She has some kind of crisis going on with her daughter. And why hasn't she introduced me to Kate, or Neil for that matter? Is she ashamed of me?'

'What does she say?'

'That she wants to get to know me first, just her and me but...'

'Maybe she's genuine.'

'Maybe. And now with Mike seeming more interested in Peggy than me, it's got me wondering.'

Linda rubbed her eyebrow. 'How so?'

'Adam's a lovely guy. He and Peg seemed so happy but now this Mike wants to sweep her off her feet. I mean, supposing he's successful?'

'From what you've said about him is she really likely to fall for his charms? He sounds arrogant.'

'Girls,' Mrs Smith called upstairs. 'It's on the table.'

'Come on.' Linda stubbed out the ciggie in a metal ashtray before helping me off her bed. 'Let's go and have something to eat. I'm starving.'

I hugged my friend. 'I knew I could rely on you.'

The table was set for three. I took a seat next to Linda. 'Thanks for letting me join you, Mrs Smith.'

'You're always welcome, dear.' She placed a plate of liver casserole, mash and cabbage in front of me. 'Are you feeling better now?'

'A little.'

Chapter Twenty-Seven

Peggy

'Tell me you're not contemplating going.' Adam marched up and down the sitting room carpet.

'Well Kate's doing much better. You've seen how she's been eating. Her plate's been clean every day for a week now. She's even making packed lunches to take to school without any prompting.'

'But...'

'He just wants us to be like a normal family going around the zoo. Why don't you come too?'

'No thanks. I've no interest in meeting him. Sounds like a right plonker to me.'

'Exactly.' I hooked my arms around his neck, swaying. 'And when, Mr Davies, have you known me to be interested in plonkers?' I chuckled and Adam joined in.

'Well don't be too long. Be home by six so we can have tea all together. We haven't done that for ages. Both Kate and Neil will be home for a change.'

'Will do.' I kissed him full on the lips. 'You've nothing to worry about. It's you I love. And remember, I'm only doing this for Rachel.'

I met Rachel at the clock tower and we walked across to The George together. 'How has it been going?'

Shaking her head, she scowled.

I stopped and held her towards me. 'What?'

'Watch yourself, Peggy. I don't think he's interested in me at all. I'm just a way for him to get back into your knickers.'

'Rachel.'

'I mean it. We had a big row yesterday and I ran out on him. To be honest, I wasn't sure whether to come today or not.'

'Listen' – I held both of her hands and looked into her eyes – 'I'm not interested in him one bit. In fact, I'm wondering what I ever saw in him. I'm only here for you.' I hugged her.

'Thanks.'

'We should get over there. He'll be waiting.' I linked arms with her.

I'd forgotten how smelly zoo animals could be as I hadn't been there since the kids were young. After gazing up at the giraffes Rachel said, 'I need to find a loo. How about you, Peggy?'

'I'm okay thanks' – I pointed to a sign – 'looks like they're that way. We'll wait for you on that bench.'

Rachel hurried along the pathway, her white patent leather handbag swinging from side to side, while Mike and I made our way to the seat. He sat closer to me than I'd have liked but I inched over as far as I could go. 'You're still as beautiful as you were all those years ago,' he whispered, brushing his fingers through my hair.

My heart beat faster against my will. I was a young girl again flattered by the attention from this American soldier. He moved his hand down from my shoulder, round to my face, stroked my cheek, and brought his lips to mine so I couldn't resist.

'What the hell?' Rachel was in front of us with her handbag aimed at Mike ready to clout him. 'What was that you were saying, Peggy?' Rachel stormed off.

I got up quickly and hurried after her. 'It's not what it looked like, I promise you. Just for a moment I let my guard down. I told you, I'm not interested in him.'

'It didn't look that way to me from where I was standing. I'm done here.' She turned to Mike who'd caught up behind us. 'You couldn't give a damn about getting to know me, could you?'

'That's not true. Calm down, sweetie.'

She slapped his face. 'Don't you bloody tell me to calm down. You come over from America with promises of wanting to get to know me as your daughter but spend all your time chasing after another man's wife. Well, I won't let you do it.' She turned back to me. 'Adam deserves better than this.'

'Yes, you're right. He does.' I faced Mike. 'And you know I'm married and let's face it if you'd really loved me, then you wouldn't have waited until now to be telling me. You'd never have given up trying to find me.'

'I didn't know how to.' He leaned towards me.

I backed away. 'Well, it's too late now. I'm happily married. At least I was until you turned up.' I flicked my hair back. 'I think we should go. Today's outing is over.'

'I agree.' Rachel hooked her arm in mine and we made our way out of the zoo towards the taxi rank.

Adam had the front door open. 'Thank God, you're back.'

'Why? What's the matter?'

'Our Kate's up in her room crying her eyes out and she won't tell me what's wrong.'

I threw my handbag down in the hallway and kicked off my shoes. 'I'll go straight up.' I dashed upstairs, hurried along the landing, stopped at Kate's bedroom and tapped on her door.

'Go away,' came from the other side.

'Kate, it's me, Mam.'

'I don't want to talk to anyone.' She sniffled.

I inched the door open wide enough to see her sobbing on the bed. 'Darling, what is it? You know you can tell me anything.' I pushed the door and rushed inside, flopped down next to her on the bed and held her in my arms. 'Baby, what is it?'

'I can't say. Mam, please, I just want to be left alone.'

'Well, I'm not leaving you alone in this state.' I rocked her in my arms. 'Is it a lad?'

'She shook her head.

'To do with your exams?'

'I don't want to talk about it.'

'All right. It's all right. You don't have to talk, just know that your mam's here for you. You're my baby and I love you dearly. It pains me to see you so sad.' Adam was right. I should spend more time at home with Kate. She needed me. I'd get those ideas of a job out of my head. I was a mam. That was my job. I held Kate in my arms until the sun went down. By that time, she'd stopped crying and drifted off to sleep. I'd tell Rachel that I couldn't see her until Mike had gone back to the States.

Chapter Twenty-Eight

Peggy

Kate grabbed her packed lunch, and an apple for breakfast, and kissed me before going off to school. She seemed to have settled down in the last few weeks. Adam and I had relaxed about her eating and convinced ourselves that she didn't have a disorder. After all, she was eating again, although I hadn't noticed signs of weight gain yet. If anything, she looked thinner. Perhaps it was because she was still growing upwards.

I'd promised Rachel to meet her for lunch. I was in town anyway as I needed to go to the shops to order the tins for Neil and Kate's birthday cakes. We were planning a small joint party with a few close friends. I loved entertaining and had so little opportunities. It was wonderful to have an excuse. I took a notebook and pencil from the top drawer in the sideboard and made my way into the sun lounge to write a list. Nuts, crisps, vol-u-vents, cheese and pineapple, sausages on sticks, a couple of black forest gateaux and then the tins for the kids' cakes. The number *one* would do for them both and a number *six* and *eight*. Kate had hit her sixteenth birthday in July and I'd made a small cake but wanted a special cake for the party. Originally, we'd planned to do the celebration in August but with the worry over Kate, we'd postponed it until closer to Neil's birthday.

The postman popping the post through the door broke my thoughts. I wandered into the hallway and picked up the brown envelopes. Bill. Another bill. Oh no, what was this? An airmail letter. Mike. I hadn't heard from him since he'd returned to the States over two months ago. Should I read it or put it straight into the bin? Curiosity got the better of me. I tore it open, unfolded the paper and scrunched it up after reading. It was a good job Adam was at work. If he saw that... There was no way I'd reply and hopefully Mike would get the message that I wasn't interested. It was time I started to put my family back together again and the birthday party was a great opportunity. I had wanted to invite Rachel but with everything that had happened of late it wasn't the right time for Kate and Neil to meet her. The clock chimed eleven. I should get ready if I was going to get into town by twelve. Rachel had made a point that I should be prompt as she only had the hour, and fifteen minutes of that was taken up walking there and back to the park.

I hurried into the kitchen and prepared two rounds of ham sandwiches, a flask of black coffee, and threw a few cherry tomatoes and sliced cucumber into a plastic container, placing everything in the cooler bag from the pantry. What did I have that was sweet? I opened the goodie cupboard and pulled out a box of Jaffa Cakes. Rachel had said they were her favourites.

I was waiting outside the newspaper office when Rachel came out of the door. She greeted me with a kiss on the cheek. 'I must be back by five-to-one.'

'I've made us a picnic as it's such a lovely day. It will save time too.'

'Cool. Thanks.' She hooked her arm in mine as we wandered across to Maple Park and stopped at a bench under an ancient oak just inside the gate. 'Do you mind if we don't go any further? That way we have a bit more time to eat and chat.'

'No. This is fine and the tree will offer us some shade. What a glorious day for September. How are you?' I asked as we sat down.

'Good thanks. I got a letter from Mike this morning. He says he's sorry for the way he behaved and hopes I'll go and visit him soon.'

'Will you?'

She shrugged. 'Might do. After all it will be a free holiday. Linda and I were supposed to book somewhere for October but with one thing and another we never got around to it. How are things with you and Adam?'

'Getting there.'

'I wish Adam was my father. He's so nice. Mike's a... well, I'm sure I don't have to tell you.'

'No, you don't. I heard from him this morning too. Begging me to come over. Said he'd send tickets for us both.'

'You're not going?'

'No. Definitely not. The letter went straight in the rubbish and I don't intend replying to him.' I took a pack of sandwiches out of the cooler bag and handed them to Rachel. 'Ham. I know you said you liked that. And there's some cherry tomatoes and sliced cucumber in here.' I pointed to the containers in the bag.

'Cheers. Thanks. Ooh are those Jaffa Cakes I spy?'

I chuckled. 'Yes, I put them in especially for you. How are things with you and Joe?'

'Good.'

'Have you thought any more about me meeting him?' I popped a cherry tomato in my mouth and it squirted everywhere. We both laughed.

'Not really,' she answered with a mouthful. 'I'll mention it to him when we meet at the weekend. I still need to tell him I'm adopted.'

'He doesn't know?' A gull flew down and stole the sandwich from my hand. 'Oi,' I shouted at it.

'They can get a bit like that. You're going to be hungry. Here' – she passed me half of hers – 'have some of mine.'

I thought about Kate and how we'd had to persuade her to eat. 'No. I'm okay, thanks. You eat it. You need to keep your strength up.'

'Oh well, if you're sure?' She stuffed the bread into her mouth. 'Can I start on the Jaffa Cakes now?'

Her eating manners were terrible. Kate and Neil hadn't had half the opportunities she'd had, yet they'd never have spoken with their mouths full or grabbed the Jaffa Cakes. Hmm, maybe that's where we'd gone wrong. Perhaps if they had then Kate wouldn't have contemplated starving herself. But that was all done with now. She was eating again.

'It's Joe's birthday next month. He'll be eighteen and I'm not sure what to get him. Any ideas?'

'What sort of thing does he like? Neil's eighteen then too. I had hoped to invite you over to meet the family but with everything Kate's been going through it isn't the right time.'

'When will be the right time, Peggy? Are you ashamed of me?'

'No, of course not. I've enjoyed it being just you and me getting to know each other. I'm sure Kate and Neil will love you too, but trust me, now is not the time.'

She scowled. 'If you say so. Anyway, what are you buying Neil for his eighteenth?'

'Maybe a watch with an engraved message on the back, or a silver tankard. Something he can keep. You should do the same. Does Joe smoke?'

'Yeah. Sometimes.'

'How about a lighter? You could get it engraved? Or a wallet?'

'Thanks, Peggy. Great ideas.' She checked her watch. 'I should get back. Do you mind if I run on?'

'No. You go. I'll see you soon. I'll have a bit of a stroll before doing my shopping.' I kissed her on the cheek and watched her dash down the path. I hoped it wouldn't be too long before I could bring her into the family. She'd be good for Kate, and for Neil.

∙∕∘

Adam opened the front door. What was he doing home at this time? 'Where've you been?'

'In town. Remember I told you I needed to order the tins for the cakes and I was meeting Rachel for lunch. Why? Where's the fire?'

'The school phoned me at work because they couldn't get hold of you. Kate's been taken to hospital.'

I leaned on the wall to steady myself. 'Oh my God. What's wrong with her?'

'I'm not sure. Are you okay? You've gone awfully pale.'

'Just feeling dizzy. Shock probably.'

'Sit down for a minute' – he helped me to the telephone seat in the hallway – 'I'll get you a glass of water. We don't want you in hospital too.' He rushed off to the kitchen and was back in seconds. 'Here. Drink this.'

'Thank you.' I sipped the water. 'We should go.' I got up, placed the glass on the shelf, and opened the front door.

Adam grabbed the keys and unlocked the car.

Adam drove into the car park, found a space, and parked. 'You feeling better now?'

'Yes,' I lied, still feeling like I was going to throw up. What was wrong with Kate? Had she had an accident? The school hadn't given Adam any information other than one of the teachers had driven her to the hospital.

We charged into the entrance and hurried over to reception. 'Our daughter's been brought in, Katherine Davies,' Adam said. 'Can you tell us where to go, please?'

The woman waded through a small filing box on the counter. 'Ah, yes, she's waiting to be assessed. Can you fill out this registration and then I'll get a porter to show you the way.' She handed Adam a pen and form.

While he was filling it in, I asked, 'Can you tell us why she's been brought in?'

'No, sorry, but once you go through the nurse or doctor will be able to explain.'

Adam dropped the pen to the desk and passed her the paper. 'Done. Can you get someone to show us now, please?'

The receptionist held up her hand and a young male porter came our way.

'This is Katherine Davies' parents. Can you show them where to go please?'

'Of course. Come this way.'

We followed him through two lots of double doors until we came to a side room. Kate was in bed with a doctor and nurse around her. Her teacher, Mrs Lord, was holding her hand. Kate didn't look up. The teacher whispered something to Kate and came over. 'Mr and Mrs Davies?'

'What happened?' I asked.

'She fainted. But after coming round she didn't look too good so we felt it was better to get her checked out.'

'How's she doing, doctor?' Adam asked.

'Let's talk in the relatives' room.' The doctor left the ward and we followed him into a room opposite. 'Do sit down. Can I get you some tea? Coffee?'

'No thank you,' Adam answered. 'Please can you just tell us what's wrong with our daughter?'

'Her teacher told you that she'd fainted. Well, when she got here, we checked out her heart rate and blood pressure, but I'm not happy with either of them. Her heart rate is too slow and blood pressure too low. She's also underweight. Little more than a skeleton. Have you noticed anything about her eating behaviour?'

'She did go through a spell of not eating but after we tackled her about it that seemed to stop. She was even keen to make her own packed lunches and her plate is always empty after dinner.' I turned to Adam. 'Isn't it?'

'That's right. We thought there was no further need to worry. Is this something to do with her not eating?'

'It could be. I need to run some more tests. If you don't mind, we'd like to keep her in.'

'Whatever you need to do, doctor.' Adam said. 'May we go in and see her?'

'Yes, but only for a short time. We're arranging to transfer her to another ward. You can wait until she's been moved and then you should go home.'

'Thank you, doctor.' I headed in to Kate's room and Adam followed me.

The phone rang and Adam answered it. 'Adam Davies speaking.'

'Who is it?' I asked.

He put his hand over the mouthpiece. 'The school.'

I assumed they were ringing to see how Kate was. 'I'll make us a cuppa.' I wandered into the kitchen and flicked the kettle on. Just as I was pouring water into the teapot, Adam came in. 'What is it?' I asked. His face had turned ashen.

'You should sit down.'

'You're worrying me now. What is it?'

He led me to the chair by the table. 'It was the Head.'

'Wanting to know how Kate was?'

'No.' He took a deep breath. 'Just when we think that things can't get any worse. You know our Kate's been taking a packed lunch to school.'

'Yes.'

'Well, she's not been eating it.'

'Of course she has. She's been making her favourite, and every day she tells me that she ate it all up.'

He shook his head. 'No, no she hasn't. Apparently, she's been storing it in her locker.'

'That's ludicrous. She wouldn't do that. They must be getting her mixed up with some other pupil.'

'No. It's Kate. Our Kate.'

'So how do they know? She's in hospital so...'

'The caretaker alerted the Head about the smell coming from the locker. When the Head opened it, they found the locker stacked to the top with mouldy sandwiches. It seems they've been in there for the whole of the summer holidays.' He ran his fingers through his hair. 'She's been pretending to eat her food, but why?'

'She must have that anorexia thing I told you about... but if that was the case then how come she's been eating toast for breakfast and emptying her plate at dinner time?'

He patted his upper lip. 'Has she though?' He rushed upstairs and I followed him into her bedroom. He opened her wardrobe, pulled out all her clothes but nothing. 'It has to be here somewhere.'

'Try the chest of drawers,' I said.

He pulled open the top drawer. 'Nothing.' He went down to the last couple of drawers. 'Bingo.'

I put my hand to my mouth and ran to the bathroom, lifted the loo lid, and threw up. By the time I got back, Adam was scooping up the smelly waste food into a bin. 'We'll need to get the disinfectant up here.'

'What's puzzling me' – Adam scratched his head – 'is why she left her sandwiches in the locker? Why not put them into a bin? It's not like they don't have plenty scattered around school.'

'I don't know. Maybe she forgot about them, or maybe she was worried her friends would see her throwing them away. Who knows what was going through her head?'

'I suppose so.'

'What I can't believe is how our Kate has become so sneaky. Lying to us like this.'

'It just isn't like her.'

'It isn't. I reckon she's worried about the exams. For Christ's sake. Why didn't she talk to me? I told her I was here for her.'

'Maybe if you'd been here instead of gadding about all the time it wouldn't have happened.'

'But, Adam, you said you supported me in meeting Rachel.'

'Yes, I did, but I thought you'd have brought her to meet the whole family. That way there wouldn't have been this big secret, but no, Peggy had to get to know her in her own time. And now look what's happened.'

'You can't blame me for this. I told Kate I was there for her. It's not my fault.' I burst into tears.

Adam wrapped his arms around me and burrowed my face into his chest. 'I'm sorry, Peg, it's not your fault. I'm just lashing out. It's none of our faults. If this is an illness then we need expert help to get her through it. Let's just hope the hospital has been a wake-up call for her. They'll explain the risks that she could kill herself. I can't believe she'd want that.'

I sobbed into Adam's chest. Our whole world had crumbled since Rachel had come into it. Was this the universe punishing me?

Chapter Twenty-Nine

Rachel

Joe and I took in the pale blue hydrangeas and lilac buddleias that were coming to an end as we meandered around the park. We marvelled at the crimson leaves on the Virginia Creeper climbing the high stone wall. It was strange being just the two of us these days. I missed the fun we'd spent with Stu and Linda, although at times it was embarrassing, like the day that woman had a go at us for snogging on the bench.

I hooked my arm in Joe's. 'There's something I need to tell you.'

He stopped and turned me to him. 'You're not going to chuck me, are you?'

'No, far from it. Let's wander over to the café and get a coffee.'

'Okay. So long as you're not going to ditch me.'

We strolled along the footpath admiring the lavender borders. Unfortunately they made my nose itch and gave me a sneezing fit. Thankfully, by the time we reached the café it had stopped. We headed inside and up to the counter. I asked the girl, who looked as if she was straight out of school, for two black coffees. Poor thing was suffering from acne. My face had looked like that from age twelve to fifteen. Thank goodness my skin was clear now.

The spotty-faced teen handed us the drinks.

'Let's sit over there.' I led Joe to two metal chairs at a small table. Once we were seated, I cleared my throat. 'I'm not sure how to tell you this so I'll just come out and say it. I'm adopted.'

Joe took a slurp of his coffee. 'Oh yeah. Why should that matter?'

I shrugged my shoulders. 'I suppose it shouldn't, at least if you've known about it for most of your life, but I only found out less than a year ago. It's made me feel less of a person so I didn't want to tell you in case you looked at me differently but...'

'It doesn't make any difference to me. You're still Rachel, the girl I'm in love with and going to marry. So why has it become important now?'

'My mother... That's my real mother...'

'Yes?'

'She wants to meet you. How do you feel about that?'

'If you like.'

'My father, he's American, came over back in June. Supposedly to get to know me but to be honest, he's a bit of a tool. That's why I wasn't able to see you much then. Although...'

'What?'

'He seemed more interested in resuming his romance with my mother. Anyway, I'm getting away from the point. My mother said she'd like to get to know you, so if that's okay with you we can meet her for dinner one evening, or go to a café, or the pub. Whichever you feel more comfortable with really.'

'I'll go with whatever you want, Rachel, and whenever, so long as you give me some notice.'

'Great.'

'Glad you've got that off your chest?'

'Yes.' I moved my chair closer to him so I could hold his hand.

He brought it up to his lips and kissed it. 'While we're being honest...'

'Are you adopted too?'

He chuckled. 'No, nothing like that but my kid sister is in hospital.'

'Oh, Joe. I'm so sorry. Hope it's nothing serious. Do you need to go?'

'No. There's not a lot I can do. And I'm not sure how serious it is.'

'That's awful for you. What's wrong with her?'

'I'm not exactly sure as Mam and Dad haven't told me. It breaks my heart seeing my little sister going through such a bad time. Mam and Dad have been besides themselves.'

'Maybe meeting my mother is not the best time for you now. What with your family problems?'

'No, I'm happy to. It could be just what I need to take my mind off things.'

'Okay. I'll sort out some possible dates and let you know.'

Chapter Thirty

Peggy

The doctor collared us as we reached Kate's room. 'Mr and Mrs Davies, I'd like to speak to you in the relatives' room please.'

My pulse throbbed. 'Has something happened?'

'No. Nothing new. I'd like to discuss our next move.' He held the door open. 'Please, sit down.'

Adam and I sat on the two-seater couch and the doctor took a chair opposite. 'Your daughter, Katherine, has some serious issues. She's suffering from an eating disorder known as anorexia nervosa.'

I nodded, my legs shaking, wondering what he was going to tell us next.

He leaned towards us. 'Now here's the problem. We can't keep Katherine here for much longer because we just don't have the space. However, what I'm proposing is that she is transferred to a special psychiatric ward where she can be monitored while receiving help.' He sighed. 'The downside is there's a waiting list.'

'How long?' Adam asked.

'It could be a few weeks, although at times a place has come through within a week. I'll refer her as an urgent case.' He took a deep breath. 'Unless you feel you can manage it at home?'

'No, no, doctor.' Adam blinked. 'We've tried managing it at home and failed. It's important we get our daughter well. We want our old Kate back. The carefree teenager, not this girl who hides food we think she's eaten.'

The doctor patted the back of Adam's hand. 'I understand, Mr Davies. I'll make the referral and we'll get her admitted as soon as possible.'

'Will she stay here until a place comes up?' Adam asked.

'That's unlikely, Mr Davies, but we'll keep her here for the time being.'

'But' – Adam looked from me to the doctor – 'how will we cope?'

'Like I said. I'll refer her as urgent. I'm sorry but once medically stable she'll become a psychiatric case and we don't have the space on this ward.' He shrugged. 'I wish we did.'

Adam nodded. 'I understand.'

'You can go in and see her now but don't stay too long as she needs rest.'

'Thank you, doctor.' I followed Adam into the small room. Our daughter was lying on her side towards the wall. 'Kate.' I rocked her arm but she ignored me.

'Kate, darling.' Adam rolled her over. 'We're not cross with you. We know this isn't your fault but we're going to get you help.'

'I don't need any help,' she whispered.

'Don't need any help. Good God, girl, do you think it's normal to starve yourself and hide your food. The school have been on because the caretaker brought the smell of your locker to the Head's attention, and don't think we haven't found the stash in your bedroom.' Adam shook his head, took a deep breath, and softened his tone. 'Sorry darling, I didn't mean to shout. Your mam and I will help you through this. The doctor's arranging for you to go to a clinic where they'll be able to monitor you and you'll be able to talk about what makes you do this. Our beautiful girl doing this to herself.' He shook his head again. 'Where the hell did we go wrong?'

I put my arms around him. 'We didn't, Adam. It's no one's fault. We'll get our beautiful girl better.'

'I'm not beautiful.' Kate turned towards us. 'I'm fat and ugly.'

Adam and I glanced at each other. How could she think she was fat when all we could see was skin and bone? I stroked her cheek. It was no use arguing with her while she was like this. We had to trust in the doctors. They would make her better again but it was going to take time.

Chapter Thirty-One

Rachel

Shouts and screams came from above the back office.

'Whatever's going on?' Betty asked.

I turned away from the telex. 'I'm not sure. Who's up there?'

'Sam and Mel, I think. Hold the fort. I'll be back shortly.'

I thought Betty had gone upstairs but she returned just as the telex message had transmitted. 'The boss is on his way up there now.'

After more shouting and heavy footsteps on the stairs, the front door slammed. Mr Strange came in to see us.

'Ladies, Mr Jeffries has been escorted from the premises and under no circumstances is he to be allowed back into the building. Is that clear?'

Betty, Mary and I nodded. Jeffries, that was Sam. What the heck had gone on upstairs?

'Mrs Jones,' Mr Strange said to Betty, 'are you able to spare, Miss Webster?'

'Yes, yes of course.'

'Miss Webster, make your way up to the staffroom and look after Miss Brown.'

'What about Lizzie, I mean Miss Carter, the receptionist?' Betty asked. 'Has she been briefed.'

'Yes, she has. Now off you go Miss Webster, take as long as necessary. Miss Carter has agreed to stay on until you're able to relieve her.'

'Yes, Mr Strange.' I hurried out of the door, along the corridor and upstairs to the staffroom. Mel was crying. I pushed the door open and rushed in. 'Mel. Whatever's happened.' I hugged her.

She sobbed on my shoulder.

'What happened?' I asked again.

She lifted her head. I gasped when spotting the swelling and discolouration around the left-hand side of her face. 'My God, did he do this?'

She nodded.

'But why?'

'He found out that I told you about, you know…'

'How?'

'It kind of slipped out in a row. I said what you'd said about him being controlling.'

I rocked her in my arms. 'Is the engagement over?'

She forced a smile. 'I hope not.'

'Surely you won't stay with him now?'

She sobbed into my chest. 'But I love him.'

'Well, I don't know whether you know or not but he's got the sack. Exactly what the bastard deserves. I told you, Mel, he's bad news and if you've got any sense, you'll break up with him. If he's doing this now before you're married then goodness knows what he'll do afterwards. You'll end up dead.'

'He didn't mean to do it.' She sobbed. 'I know he didn't.'

I shook my head. There was no reasoning with the girl. I couldn't understand how she could even contemplate staying with someone who had hurt her.

I knocked on Mr Strange's office. 'Come in,' he called.

'Sorry to disturb you, sir, but Miss Brown's in a bit of a bad way. I wondered if you'd like me to take her home?'

'No, but thank you, Miss Webster, I'll take her home myself. You get back to work. I imagine Miss Carter's waiting to be relieved.'

'Yes, Mr Strange.'

He followed me out of the office and made his way upstairs to the staffroom. I headed for reception. 'Sorry you had to stay late, Lizzie,' I said, 'but you can go now.'

'But what about your lunch?'

'No, worries. I'll eat my sandwich during a quiet moment.'

'If you're sure. Thanks. What's been going on up there?'

'Sam...' I stopped when I heard footsteps on the stairs. 'I'll tell you in a minute.'

The boss led Mel to reception. She had covered her face with a headscarf. 'Miss Webster,' Mr Strange said, 'can you pop to the back office and get Miss Brown's belongings please?'

'Yes, sir.' I hurried through to the back office. Betty had gone home and Mary was on the switchboard. She glanced up while taking a call. I grabbed Mel's handbag and rushed back. 'Here you are, Mel. Phone me later if you need me.'

'Thank you, Miss Carter, for staying behind,' Mr Strange said. 'I'm driving Miss Brown home. Would you like a lift too as we've kept you late?'

'No, I'm fine thank you, sir. I have my bicycle in the car park.'

'Very well. Have a good weekend.' He turned to me. 'Once I'm back, Miss Webster, you can go for your lunch.'

'Thank you, Mr Strange.'

'Come along, Miss Brown.' He closed the door behind them.

'What happened?' Lizzie asked again.

'Seems like our Sam's been a bit too heavy with his fists. Poor Mel's going to have a whopping black eye. Goodness knows how bad it'll get. And would you believe she's not even considering breaking off the engagement.'

'I think her folks might have something to say about that.' Lizzie looked up at the clock. 'I'd better go.'

⤝

Joe was outside when I finished work.

'Joe, what are you doing here?'

'I'm really sorry, Rach, but I can't make tonight. You remember I mentioned my sister not being well…?'

'Yes?'

'Well, she's been discharged from hospital so Mam and Dad have asked me if I can stay in tonight. We're having some kind of family meeting. I'm really sorry.'

I put my arms around him. 'Go. I'll be fine. I'll see if Linda fancies a girlie night in. You know, hair, make-up, that sort of thing.'

'Thanks, babe.' He kissed me on the lips before hurrying over to his motorbike. I thought it was strange how his sister was poorly and my half-sister wasn't well either. Must be something in the water striking young girls down. I crossed over the road to Woolies where Mr Peters and Linda were locking up.

'Good evening, Miss Webster.' Mr Peters clicked the padlock at the bottom of the doors. 'How are you getting on at the newspaper office?'

'Brilliant, thank you. I really love it there.'

'Good news. Good news. Well, ladies, I bid you goodnight. I'll see you in the morning, Miss Smith. Nice to see you again, Miss Webster.' Mr Peters ambled down the road swinging a gentleman's brolly by his side.

Once he was out of earshot I said, 'Always prepared, our Mr Peters.'

Linda laughed. 'This is a nice surprise but what are you doing here?'

'Joe had to cancel on me so I wondered whether you fancied a girlie evening as we haven't had one for a while?'

'Sure. Want to stay for tea?'

'If that's okay with your mam.'

'She'll be fine. You know you're always welcome at ours.'

I wished I could say the same to her. 'Then yes I'd love to but I'd best telephone home to let Mum know, otherwise she'll cook dinner for me.'

'Sure, we can do that on the way.'

Halfway to Linda's the heavens opened. It seemed Mr Peters had the right idea with a brolly. We put our handbags on our heads while running down the path and on reaching the red phone box we charged in. I made the quick call and once I'd replaced the receiver looked outside at the pouring rain. 'I suppose we could shelter in here?'

'Yeah.'

We giggled as lightning hit the sky and the next minute a crash of thunder made us jump. An old woman bashed on the glass. 'You girls finished?' She opened the door. 'If you've finished your call then I need to use the phone urgently.'

I shoved Linda out. 'Sorry,' I said to the old woman. 'Hope everything's okay.'

She grunted, pushing past us into the kiosk.

'Yum, that was lovely,' I said to Mrs Smith when placing my cutlery down on the plate. 'Shepherd's pie's my favourite. Would you like us to wash up?'

'No, you girls go and have some fun.'

'Thanks.' I followed Linda upstairs to her bedroom. 'Your mam's so nice.' I remembered all the lies Linda had said about her mam in the past but since she'd been having counselling everything seemed better in the Smith household.

While messing around doing makeovers on each other I told Linda all about what had happened with Sam and Mel. 'He's a nasty piece of work. Why do some women let men treat them like that?'

Linda twitched. 'I suppose they love them and hope that things will change.'

'They never do though. Another strange thing. Joe's sister has just come out of hospital. Strange because my half-sister is the same age and she's been poorly too. Do you think it's to do with exam stress?'

'Might be.' She held a vanity mirror in front of me. 'What do you think?'

'Um, I look different with the plum colour lippie but I like it.' I grinned into the mirror.

'Have it. I'll pick up another one tomorrow at work.'

'Thanks, Lind.' I hugged her. 'You're the best.'

'I know' – she prodded the top of my arm – 'and don't you forget it.'

Chapter Thirty-Two

Peggy

Adam parked the car in the drive. I got out of the back and walked around to the other side to help Kate. My eyes blurred as I looked at my once beautiful daughter.

Without a word she got out and hurried up to the open front door. Once inside she went to go upstairs but Adam pulled her back.

'Not yet, love. Your mam and I want to talk to you.'

She twisted herself from his grip. 'There's nothing to say. I've got work to do. I'm already behind.'

He held her in his arms. 'That can wait. The school know you're not well.'

'You just want me to fail,' she shouted, escaping from his hold and charging straight upstairs.

Adam shook his head. 'How are we going to cope? Let's hope they get a space for her soon.'

'Let's hope so,' I said, 'but in the meantime we need to ensure she eats all meals downstairs, and we should speak to Neil about watching her too. It's not right he doesn't know what's going on.'

Adam patted my arm. 'You're right, Peg. Let's put the kettle on and have a cuppa and see if we can work out a plan.'

We wandered into the kitchen. I filled the kettle and flicked the switch while Adam scooped three heaped spoons of tea into the pot. 'I don't know about you, Peg,' he said, 'but I'm starving. Shall I pop down the road and get us fish and chips after this?'

My stomach rumbled. 'That sounds like a good idea and you never know we may be able to tempt Kate to eat a bit. Before this, she always loved a chippie tea.' The kettle boiled so I added the water to the pot and stirred it. 'Do you remember how she always used to ask for mushy peas?'

Adam gave a small laugh. 'I do. I remember when she called them mussy peas because she couldn't say mushy. Do you?'

'Yes, but even funnier when she asked for fizz'n'pips.' I poured tea and milk into two mugs. 'Let's take these into the other room. I could do with a comfy seat.'

Adam followed me into the lounge. We placed our teas down on the coffee table and flopped onto the settee. He put his arm around me. 'How are we going to get through this?'

'We will. The psychiatric clinic will help. The doctor said he'll get her a place urgently.' As I snuggled up close to Adam the front door opened and closed and Neil strolled in.

'Hiya. You two look cosy.'

'We're just having a quick cuppa.' I sat upright. 'The tea's warm in the pot. How do you feel about fizz'n'pips for dinner?'

He roared with laughter. 'Isn't that what our Kate used to say when she was younger? Speaking of Kate. Where is she?'

'Up in her room. Get yourself a cuppa and come and sit down. Your dad and I would like to tell you what's been going on.'

'Will do.' He left the room and was back in minutes with a mug of tea. He plonked himself in an armchair. 'So, what is it? She's not got cancer, has she?'

'No, nothing like that,' Adam answered in almost a whisper. 'She's got something called anorexia nervosa. An eating disorder.'

Neil gasped. 'Is that why she's so thin?'

I nodded.

'Phew thank goodness. Then all we have to do is make her eat. Simple.' He took a gulp of his tea.

'If only it was that simple,' I said. 'She thinks she's fat.'

'Oh my God. How can she think that? She's like a walking skeleton. So why can't we just make her eat more?'

Adam covered his mouth and mumbled behind his fist, 'She's been hiding her food.'

'What? How?'

'At home, in her bedroom, and at school in her locker,' I said. 'This is where you come in, Neil. We're going to need all eyes on her to stop her sneaking food from her plate upstairs. The doctor at the hospital is making a referral for her to be admitted into a psychiatric ward but we don't know how long that will take.'

Neil shook his head. 'I don't get it. Why? Why's this happened to her now?'

'We don't know.' Adam picked up his drink and took a sip. 'And we need to speak quietly because we don't want her to know we're talking about her. It could be the stress of exams or it could be because your mam's not been around as much the last few months.'

I flinched. So, he was still blaming me, despite him saying it was no one's fault. Was it my fault? 'We're hoping she'll get a place in the ward in the next week or so,' I said, 'and as soon as she starts treatment the sooner she can start getting well again. It may mean that we'll have to cancel your birthday party.'

Neil flicked his hand. 'That's not important. What's important is that my kid sister gets better. I can't believe this, but at least it's not a life-threatening disease.'

Adam nodded. 'It could be. That's why we all need to be vigilant.'

'And that's why we're having fizz'n'pips for tea,' I said, trying to make light of things. 'We're hoping she won't be able to resist.'

Neil gulped the rest of his drink down. 'Would you like me to go for them now?'

'If you don't mind.' Adam got up from the settee and made his way to the sideboard to get his wallet.' He pulled out a tenner. 'Get four cod and chips. Oh, and if they've got mushy peas get some of them too. She used to love them.'

Neil waved the note. 'Shan't be long.'

Chapter Thirty-Three

Rachel

Linda held the vanity mirror up to me. 'Have a gander.'

My hair shone. Soft bouncy waves framed my face. 'I love it. Your turn now.'

She perched on the edge of her bed and I unrolled the curlers from her hair. Auburn locks flowed loose to her shoulders in a style similar to mine.

'You look gorgeous.' I passed her the mirror.

'Let's go and have a peep in Mam's room and then we can see what the back looks like.'

'Won't she mind?'

'Nope. I do it all the time. Come on.' Linda charged next door to Mrs Smith's bedroom and I followed. She sat down at the dressing table. 'Here.' She passed me the vanity mirror. 'Hold that at the back so I can see what it looks like.'

I did as she instructed.

She put a hand to the nape of her neck. 'It's fab. Do you think Stu will be able to resist me?'

'I hope not.' How could Stu resist her with that gorgeous red hair and sparkling eyes? Joe and I had convinced him to give their relationship another go. *One date*, he'd said, *I'm not promising more than that*. I felt they were meant to be. Just like Joe and me.

Linda rushed back to her room with me in tow. She stepped into the green satin mini dress that matched her eyes.

'You look stunning.'

'Thanks. I'll just go and check. Come on.' She hurried back to her mam's bedroom and stood on the bed to check her outfit in the dressing table mirror. When she stepped down, she said, 'Go on. Your turn.'

'On your mam's bed?'

'Yep. She won't mind.'

I climbed onto the bed and peered in the mirror at my white gypsy blouse and chocolate cheesecloth maxi skirt.

'You look cool.'

'Cheers.' I got down from the bed and straightened the pink satin bedspread. I wondered what my mum and dad would say if I stood on their bed to check my outfits. Although there was no need to wonder as I already knew.

Linda sat on the stool at the vanity unit and traced plum lippie across her lips. Afterwards she sprayed Charlie on her wrists and under her neck. 'Want some?'

'Yes, go on. I forgot to bring mine.'

She squirted me with the perfume and I sniffed my wrists. 'Mmm, nice. I hope Joe likes it. He's used to me wearing Gingham.'

'Good to have a change then. Come on, move your arse, and let's go, otherwise we'll be late.'

We slipped matching bottle green and burgundy striped ponchos over our heads that we'd picked up from the market last week.

Linda and I jumped off the bus and made our way to The Black Horse. When we got to the entrance, Linda held back. She held out her hands. 'Look, I'm shaking. Supposing he doesn't want me?'

'You'll never know if we don't go in.'

'But' – she clung to my arm – 'I'm not sure I can face it. You know what happened when he chucked me.'

'You're stronger now and having counselling. Anyway, you look gorgeous. He won't be able to resist you.' I tugged at her arm and shoved her through the door. 'Walk.'

She gripped my hand as we made our way to the back of the pub. As we got close to Stu and Joe's table, Stu's eyes lit up.

'Look. He's pleased to see you. Go on.' I pushed her forward.

Stu rose from the table. 'It's good to see you, Lind. You look well. What can I get you to drink?'

'Half a cider please.'

'Woodpecker?'

'Yes, please.' Her bright green eyes twinkled.

'And what about you, Rachel?' Stu asked.

'I'll have the same.'

Joe got up from his seat and gave me a quick kiss on the lips. 'Hi, gorgeous. Looks like our Stu's smitten.'

'Let's hope so,' I whispered.

He moved over to Stu. 'I'll come and help get the drinks. Any crisps for the ladies, or peanuts?'

'Peanuts would be great.' I slid along the bench seat next to Linda leaving the chairs opposite for the lads. 'See,' I said, 'he still likes you and I reckon he's as nervous as you too.'

Linda smiled. She was much quieter than her normal self. 'Joe looks a bit haggard.'

'I was thinking that. His sister's out of hospital now.'

'That's good. How about your half-sister? Is she any better?'

'I don't think so as I've not seen Peggy for a couple of weeks. She said she can't leave home at the moment. Shh,' I said, 'here they come.'

'It's like old times.' Joe took out a pack of Woodbines. 'Ciggie, Linda?'

'Thanks.'

Stu struck a match and Linda took a drag on the cigarette to get it to light.

'Rach?' Joe passed them to me.

'No, thanks. I've decided to give up.'

'Good idea. Maybe I should do that too. It would certainly save a bit of cash.'

I reached across the table to take Joe's hand. "You look tired. Is your sister still poorly?'

'She's getting there,' he said.

'What did you say was wrong?'

'Er, I'm not quite sure what Mam said it was. I don't think it's too serious though.'

Linda downed her drink. 'I need the loo. Will you come with me, Rach?'

'Sure.' I kissed Joe. 'I'll be back in a minute.'

We wandered out of the pub to the almost black. I took a torch from my bag and pointed the glow at the ground so we could see where we were going. 'Thanks for coming with me,' Linda said when we reached the toilets. 'I wondered what you thought about Stu. You reckon he's in to me?'

'Definitely.' I shivered. 'I hate coming in here in case of spiders. Wish they'd update their facilities to indoor. Mind you, at least the light bulbs are working this evening. Last week they weren't. Now I always make sure I carry a torch.'

'Good idea. Right, I'd better go for a quick wee.' She slipped into the cubicle.

'Don't be long then. Like I said, I don't like it in here.' I checked my lippie in the small mirror on the wall, and adjusted my off the shoulder broderie anglaise blouse while absurd thoughts ran through my head. I waited until Linda came out and asked, 'Don't you think it's a bit strange that these two sixteen-year-old girls are both ill at the same time?'

She shrugged her shoulders. 'Not really. Like you say it could be to do with exam stress. Of course, what do I know as I left school without taking any. Did you get ill?'

'No.'

'How about your Jen?'

'No, but she did say someone at college had been off sick for a while.'

'There you go then. Nothing strange at all. Just a coincidence and coincidences happen all the time.'

'Yep, just me being silly.'

By the time we'd got back in, Stu had been up to the bar to grab the darts. It was like old times as Joe and I played against Linda and Stu. Once Joe and I had won the game he looked up at the clock. 'I should get back home. If you need me to give you a lift, Rach, you'll have to come now.'

I glanced at Linda and she nodded *okay*.

'Yes please, Joe.' I kissed Linda on the cheek and whispered, 'Don't do anything I wouldn't do.'

She giggled. 'Hopefully.'

Before leaving, we turned back and glimpsed at our friends in each other's arms.

'It looks like they're back together.' I took Joe's hand as we left the pub.

The weather had suddenly turned, it was wet, cold and windy. My umbrella kept blowing inside out so I was glad when I reached Elmo's. I pushed open the door, collapsed my brolly, and popped it in the stand by the entrance. The warmth from the café's heaters welcomed me. I spotted Linda at a table near the back, waved and strode over.

'You look a bit wet.' She pushed a hot chocolate close to me. 'Took the liberty of getting the drinks in. Thankfully I got in before that huge downpour.'

'Cheers.' I took off my dripping raincoat and hung it on the spare chair. 'So, what's the plan? Shopping? I still need to find something for Joe's birthday.'

'Think it'll have to be. We can hardly go walking around the park in this weather. Not the best day for me to have taken as a holiday. I had to fight to get the Saturday off too.'

'Never mind. We'll make it fun.' I took a sip from the hot chocolate. 'Mmm, just what I needed. Anyway, never mind that, how did things go with you and Stu last night after we left?'

She grinned. 'A lady never tells.'

'You didn't?'

'I might have.'

'It's official then. You're back together.'

'We are. And we have you and Joe to thank for that.'

'That deserves a toast.' I raised my cup. 'To Lind and Stu.'

'To me and Stu.' She laughed.

Life was looking good. I had my best friend back and things were even better at home. I hadn't had a row with Mum or Dad for weeks, although I hadn't told them that Linda and me were friends again. Instead, when seeing her I'd let them think I was out with Joe or Mel.

Linda gulped the last of her hot chocolate. 'Shall we brave the shops then?'

I peered out of the window. 'It looks like it's stopped raining at least. We just need to make sure we don't get blown away. I can't believe how the weather has suddenly changed.'

'Hmm. It is almost October. What do you expect?'

'Suppose so.' I got up from the table and slid my arms into my raincoat.

'You going to be okay walking around the shops in them?' She pointed to my white PVC boots.

'Yeah. They're really comfy.' I slung my matching handbag across my shoulder. 'Let's go.'

Mum opened the oven and took out a joint of lamb. 'It's nice to have you in for Sunday lunch for a change. Not seeing Joe today?'

'No. He needs to stay at home for his sister. She's not been well.'

'He's a good family boy. Hope we get to see him again soon. Bring the vegetables, will you?'

I picked up the dish of carrots and peas and followed Mum into the dining room. Dad was already at the table so she put the joint in front of him to carve.

'Well, this is nice,' he said, 'the whole family together for lunch. It's been a while.'

Mum returned with a tray of roast potatoes and the gravy boat. 'Where's Jennifer?'

'I think she's finishing off an assignment. Shall I get her?' I smiled.

'If you don't mind.' Mum positioned the white napkins on the table.

As I left the room Dad whispered, 'It's wonderful to see how she's settled down these last few months. For a while there I thought we'd lost her.'

I wanted to continue to stand outside the door and listen to Mum's answer but thought I'd be a bit conspicuous. It was enough that we had harmony in the household. It had been awful for all of us. Of course, I knew if I told them about Linda everything would change so I kept shtum.

'Jen,' I called from the landing, 'lunch is on the table.'

'Coming.'

I dashed downstairs and into the dining room and took my seat. 'She's on her way.'

Within seconds Jenny was at the table next to me. 'Roast lamb. My favourite. I'm starving.'

Above the clatter and clang of crockery, as we served potatoes and vegetables onto our plates, Mum asked me, 'Did you manage to get Joe his present?'

'No, not yet. I've got some ideas though. There's still a couple of weeks before I need to worry.'

'Your father and I would like to get him a little gift too, as it's his eighteenth. Do you think that would be all right?'

I scooped a teaspoon of mint sauce on to my meat. 'I don't see why not. What were you thinking?'

'Nothing too grand, obviously, but possibly an engraved photograph frame or tankard.'

'That sounds nice. Peggy reckons she might get Neil an engraved tankard. Remember I told you he's eighteen too.'

'But you've not met your other sister and brother yet?' Dad took a sip of red wine.

'No. Apparently Kate's not been too well so Peggy felt we should wait a while.' Mum and Dad appeared keen. Perhaps it was time to tell them about our engagement. 'Actually' – I put my knife and fork down on the side of my plate – 'there's something I've been meaning to tell you all.' I pulled the necklace from under my jumper, unclicked the catch and slipped the ring off the chain and onto my finger. 'Joe and I are engaged.'

Dad slammed his cutlery down. 'What the hell do you mean, you're engaged? For God's sake, girl, you're only just nineteen.'

'And old enough to decide.'

'The boy's not even eighteen' – Dad glared at me – 'he's still a minor. What do his parents say about this charade?'

'They don't know yet. I don't know why you're carrying on like this, it's not like we're planning to get married for at least another couple of years. I thought you liked Joe.'

'We do, darling,' Mum said, 'but you're too young to be engaged and you've not known him long.'

Dad shot up from his chair. 'Are you sleeping with him? Is that why? They say the apple never falls far from the tree.' He clung to his chest. 'Rosalind, quick, get my spray.'

Mum took the spray from his jacket pocket and handed it to him. 'Take it easy, Charles.'

'You're disgusting if you think that.' I pushed my plate away and got up from the table. 'I knew I shouldn't have told you. I hate you both.' I stormed out of the room and stood outside for a moment to listen.

'Are you all right, Charles?' Mum asked.

'I will be.' Dad said in a calm voice.

'What was that we were saying about no arguments?' Mum said.

Chapter Thirty-Four

Peggy

'Will you be back by the time I get home?' Neil asked as he left the table.

'We should be.' Adam folded the newspaper. 'Have you said goodbye to your sister?'

'Yeah, although she wasn't very responsive. She will be okay, won't she?'

'This is the best thing for her,' I said. 'As soon as she starts the treatment the sooner we'll get our old Kate back. And we can go and see her. She'll need us.'

'I'd best get off to college. Hope it goes well. See you later.'

'Don't forget your packed lunch,' Adam said.

'Thanks for the reminder, Dad.' Neil took the Tupperware box from the fridge and headed out. 'Ta-ra.' The front door slammed.

'We should get her out of bed in a few minutes,' I said to Adam. 'How do you think she'll react?'

'Who knows? But this is the right thing to do and we're lucky the doctor managed to get her an emergency place.'

'Yes.' I felt bad because I had to put off seeing Rachel the last couple of weeks but Kate needed me, although so did Rachel, just not in the same way. Thank goodness I didn't have to worry about Neil. He spent most of his time around the house whistling when he was at home and he always had a big smile on his face. I was sure he must have a girlfriend. Once Kate was on the road to recovery, we should sit down with Neil and find out more. If there was a girlfriend we'd invite her over for tea.

Adam put the breakfast dishes by the sink. 'Are you going up to Kate or would you like me to?'

'She might take it better from you. You know what a Daddy's girl she is.'

'Was,' he said.

'Why don't you give it a go while I wash the dishes?'

'If you're sure?'

'Yes, I'm sure.' I was a nervous wreck if the truth was to be told but then so was he. We just wanted our carefree girl back again. Both Adam and I had lost weight these last few weeks from worry. We'd tried to eat properly to set a good example but it was hard when feeling torn inside. I squirted a drop of Fairy Liquid into the sink and ran the hot water.

'Peg,' Adam called, 'I think I need your help.'

I wiped my hands on the towel and hurried upstairs. 'What is it?'

Adam was leaning on the banister. 'She says she's not going.'

'Well, she doesn't have any choice.'

'I'll finish the washing up. See you downstairs.'

'Okay.' I barged into Kate's bedroom. 'Get up young lady. There is no, *I'm not going*, you are. Don't let me have to make your father drag you out of bed. Up now.'

She cowered.

'I said, up.'

'I don't want to go. Please, don't make me.'

I pulled back the covers. 'Out. We're doing this for your own good. We want our old Kate back. Now I know you can't help what you've been doing to yourself but please, for once, think about your father and me. Now get up.'

She slid out of bed. I threw a pair of brown elasticated trousers and a green jumper over the back of a chair. 'Get dressed.' I left the room but went inside ours so I could listen and make sure she was moving around. The bathroom door slammed shut. After a while she pulled the chain and I heard running water. Minutes later the bathroom door re-opened and Kate returned to her own room. I crept out of mine and went downstairs to find Adam. 'She's getting dressed.'

Adam drove the Cortina into the hospital car park. He got out of the vehicle and took Kate's bag from the boot. I stepped from the passenger seat and opened the back door. 'Come on, darling.' I held out my hand.

The look of terror on Kate's face almost made me ask Adam to take us back home but I knew this was the only way. If we didn't get her well, we could lose her. 'It'll be all right. I promise you. We just want to make you better.'

'Please, Mam, don't make me. I promise I'll eat.'

'It's all right,' I said again.

Adam was at my side. 'Come along, Kate. It won't be as bad as you think. It's just a hospital. They're not going to lock you up. You'll be free to move around and able to do your schoolwork so you won't get behind.'

Finally, she slid from the car at a snail's pace and gripped my hand. 'Don't leave me, Mam.'

My stomach churned. I felt like I was walking my daughter to the gallows. It seemed an age before we got to the entrance. Adam went to reception to find out where the ward was. He returned and said, 'This way.'

We followed him into the lift, down the corridor, and around the corner until we came to Buttercup Ward. Kate dragged her heels trying to avoid going in.

'Mr and Mrs Davies?' a sister on the nurses' station asked. 'And this must be young Katherine.'

'Yes,' Adam answered, 'although she likes to be known as Kate. We have her things. She's brought some schoolwork too.'

'Doctor would like a word with you both. I'll give her a call to let her know you're here.' She picked up the telephone receiver and dialled. 'Doctor Winter, The Davies have arrived.' Sister replaced the phone and looked up at us. 'She'll be out in a couple of minutes.'

Before either of us could thank her, an attractive woman with soft blonde curls, in a straight tweed suit came into the ward. 'Mr and Mrs Davies.' She shook our hands in turn. 'And Katherine, I'm pleased to meet you, dear. No need to be frightened. Everyone is friendly here.'

I smiled. 'It's Kate.' I put an arm around my daughter.

'Of course. Well, Kate needs to go through an admission process so let's leave her with Sister and if you could come into my office?'

'Mam' – Kate clung to my arm – 'please don't leave me.'

The sister prised Kate's hand from me. 'Come along, pet. Your mam and dad will be allowed to see you before they go.'

Tears filled her eyes and I could feel mine becoming teary too. 'We'll be back soon, darling,' I said as we were led away by Doctor Winter. We turned left out of the ward and after a couple of yards followed her into a small office. Was she even qualified? She looked like a young Marilyn Monroe.

'Sit down, please. Can I get you a coffee?'

'No thank you,' I answered, and Adam said the same.

'Okay, I'll get to the point. Sister will weigh and measure Kate, and ask her a few questions. Nothing for you to worry about. We'll get her settled in and tomorrow she'll start therapy. She'll attend one-to-ones, group classes, and workshops. She won't be locked up or anything like that. We're here to make your daughter well again.'

'Thank you.' I clasped my hands together. 'She's brought some schoolwork to ensure she doesn't fall behind.'

'We do allow patients to have schoolwork, but for the first week, if you don't mind, I'd like her to concentrate on her therapy and rest. There's a television in the ward if she needs a bit of evening recreation before bed.'

'Oh, I see.' I blinked. 'I was hoping she wouldn't be in here too long.'

'There's no knowing exactly how long your daughter will take to respond. Some take weeks, others longer, but what I can tell you is it will take more than one week.'

'Are we able to visit?' Adam asked.

'Yes, of course. Visiting times are half-past six to half-past eight in the evenings Monday to Friday and two to four at weekends. But again, I'd suggest you wait at least a week before coming. You may bring family games to play in the dayroom.'

I nodded. 'We have a son. Will he be allowed to visit?'

'Yes.' She smiled. Cherry coloured lipstick emphasised her gleaming white teeth. 'I'm sure seeing her brother will help enormously with recovery. Do you have any other questions?'

I glanced at Adam. He answered, 'I don't think so. Is it all right if we go in and see our daughter now?'

'Yes, you may. But please, just say goodbye. Don't hang around as that will make Kate more anxious. The best thing we can all do is get her settled into a routine as quickly as possible.' She stood up away from the desk. 'Please, don't worry. We'll keep in touch. Feel free to phone anytime.' She passed us a business card. 'The number's direct to this ward so you don't have to go through reception.'

'Thank you.' Adam rose from the chair and helped me up and we left her office hand in hand, taking a slow pace back to the ward, frightened of what we may encounter when we arrived.

Chapter Thirty-Five

Rachel

Betty took her handbag from the cupboard and came over to me. 'That's me for another week. Have a good weekend, duck.' She lifted my hand. 'What's this? When did this happen?'

'A while ago but I've been wearing the ring on a necklace around my neck until I'd told my folks.'

'Congratulations. I take it you've told them now if you're wearing the ring? Are they happy for you?'

I started crying.

'Oh dear' – she dropped the bag and put her arm around me – 'I hadn't meant to make you cry.'

I wiped my eyes with the back of my hand. 'It's not your fault.' I snivelled. 'It seemed the right time to tell them as they really liked him and were talking about buying him a birthday present, but when I made the announcement, Dad went ballistic. Well, they can't stop me as I'm nineteen.'

'They'll just be looking out for their little girl. Don't be too hard on them. I'm sorry, darling, but I must go.' She picked up her bag. 'Look after yourself. And go for lunch.'

'I will.' I tidied up the papers on my desk and placed them in the relevant files.

I rushed across to Oasis to meet Peggy. She waved from a table by the window, I strode over and kissed her on the cheek. 'It seems ages since we last got together.'

'Yes, I'm sorry about that. But...'

'How's Kate?'

'She's doing well.'

'What did you say was wrong with her?'

'I didn't. Sorry, Rachel, but I'd rather not talk about it. Do you mind?'

I shrugged. 'Whatever.'

'I see you're wearing the ring. Does that mean your mam and dad know about your engagement?'

'Unfortunately, yes, and they didn't take it too well. They can't stop me though. It's not like we were planning to run off and get married in a hurry. I want to wait for at least a couple of years, so I really didn't see what the big deal was.'

A young waitress came to the table. 'What can I get you?'

'Beans and toast for me. Peggy?'

'Yes, I'll have the same. And two black coffees.'

'On white or brown?' The girl blinked.

'White please.' I folded up the menu.

'The same for me.' Peggy smiled.

'Will it be long?' I asked. 'Only I'm on my lunch break.'

'Shouldn't take longer than a few minutes.' The girl disappeared into the kitchen.

'What other news do you have?' Peggy blew her nose.

'Have you got a cold?'

'No. At least I hope not. I think it's this cold weather.'

'Stu and Linda are back together.'

'That's excellent. Wasn't she having counselling?'

'Yes. And it's like having the old Linda back again. Mel's okay but' – I shook my head – 'she's no fun like Linda. Anyway, she and Sam have split up. Did I tell you he started thumping her?'

'I'm not sure. So much has been going on at home that my memory isn't working at its best.'

'Two beans on toast.' A young chap in a chef's hat placed the plates in front of us.

'That was nice and quick. Thank you.' I rubbed my stomach and said to Peggy, 'I'm starving. I overslept this morning so had to miss breakfast.'

Her mouth shot open like she was going to say something.

'Are you all right? Have I said something wrong?'

'No, not at all. You shouldn't miss breakfast though.'

The young waitress was at our table. 'Two black coffees. Sorry for the delay but I had problems with the machine.'

'That's all right, dear,' Peggy answered before the girl left our table.

As I tucked into my meal I said, 'Well I was telling you about Sam and Mel. She wanted to keep seeing him but once her parents found out what had been going on, thankfully they managed to make her see sense.'

'Thank goodness for that.'

'So, when's a good time for you to meet Joe? It would be nice to have one mother who was happy for us.'

'Next week or the week after should be fine. Saturday or Sunday evening.'

'Cool. I'll sort it out.' I scraped the last of the beans onto my fork.

After the film we trundled out of the flicks. *The Godfather* hadn't been something I particularly liked but Stu and Joe seemed to have enjoyed it. We headed for *The Six Bells* as it was just around the corner. Linda and I went up to the bar and ordered the drinks.

'I'll bring them over.' The blond barman winked.

Linda and I chuckled as we made our way to the table. 'He's almost old enough to be our dad.' Linda giggled.

'Was Ed trying to chat you girls up?' Stu said.

'Well, he winked,' I said, 'but, I'm not sure whether he was really trying to come on to us.'

Stu laughed. 'He wasn't. He was just being nice. Ed's my cousin.'

'Oh shucks.' Linda slapped the table. 'I thought I'd pulled.' She snuggled into Stu. It was so nice to see them fully at ease with each other again.

I huddled up to Joe. 'My mother's ready to meet you. She can do next Saturday or Sunday evening or the week afterwards.'

'Sounds cool. Have you thought where?'

'No, not really, but as it's an evening probably best to go to a pub. This one's quite nice and at least it has indoor loos.'

Ed brought across the drinks. 'Bitters for the men and cider for the ladies.' He playfully punched Stu. 'How you doing, cuz?'

'Far out, man. You met my girl?'

'Yeah. She's rather cute, you lucky dude.' Ed patted Stu on the back. 'Have a good evening, girls.' He winked at us again.

'Where were we?' I said to Joe.

'You were asking about where we should meet your mother.' He took a slurp from his pint glass.

'Ah yes. Here?'

'Sure. I don't mind.'

How about your birthday as that's next Sunday?'

Joe's smile dropped. 'I'd rather hoped we four could do something then.'

'Of course, silly me. How about the Saturday then?'

'Probably better if you make it the following week. Sunday after my birthday? As we may wish to do something on the Saturday for Halloween?'

'You do want to meet her?'

'If I must.' He held his hands out in front and pretended to make them shake. 'Of course I want to meet her.' He laughed.

'And then I'll meet your parents if you like?'

He bit his lip. 'Let's see how things are at home by then.' He put his arm around me. 'If you don't mind.'

'No, sure. I understand. I'll tell my mother Sunday 29th October then. About seven o'clock?'

'Works for me.'

Chapter Thirty-Six

Peggy

We hovered outside the ward waiting for the bell to ring at two. Poor Neil, not exactly the best way to celebrate his eighteenth, but he'd insisted he wanted to spend some time with Kate on his birthday.

A nurse opened the double doors. 'You can come in now.'

A hoard of visitors hurried in and rushed to their loved ones. Neil headed over to Kate who was perched on her bed reading. Adam and I held back to allow our children a moment.

Neil kissed his sister on the cheek. 'How you feeling, kid?'

Kate put her book down on the bedside cabinet. 'Getting there.' She prodded his arm. 'Happy Birthday, you.'

'Thanks. What's the book?'

'*All Creatures Great and Small.* You read it?'

'Nah. The only books I seem to read these days are British Leyland manuals.'

Adam pulled up some plastic chairs. 'How's our baby girl?'

'Much better, Dad. I can't wait to come home.'

I took a seat next to Adam. 'Has the doctor said anything?'

'Hopefully, soon.' She beamed.

Neil bumped fists with his sister. 'That's the best birthday present I could have.'

'Did she give you an idea when?' I asked.

'No. But she did say soon. And if I keep doing as well... Who knows I could be home by November.'

I squeezed her fingers. 'I hope so, darling.'

Adam shook the carrier bag in his hand. 'Shall we head over to the dayroom so your brother can open his pressies?'

'Yes. Definitely.' Kate grinned.

'That sounds like a plan,' I said, 'but before we do, we've brought more schoolwork from your teacher.'

'Just leave them there.' She pointed to the locker, before climbing off the bed and heading to the dayroom arm in arm with Neil.

I stuffed the books into the small cupboard. 'Dare I believe she's put on weight?' I asked Adam.

'It does look like she's gained a few pounds, although difficult to tell with the baggy jumper she's wearing. Let's hope this nightmare is almost over.'

I gripped his hand. 'Remember what they said though. Even once she's discharged, we'll need to watch her as some patients slip back.'

'We will. Come on, let's have a bit of normal family time for a change.'

On joining the kids, I passed a small parcel to Kate and whispered, 'This is what you asked us to sort out.'

She handed the present to Neil. 'Happy birthday, big bro. I suppose that makes you an adult now?'

'Not sure I'll ever be grown-up.' He laughed. 'I reckon I'm like Peter Pan.' He ripped off the wrapping. 'A leather wallet. Groovy. I love it.'

She nudged him. 'Open it.'

He unfastened the clasp and spotted the fiver in the note compartment. 'You know what, Kate, I'm going to save this until you're discharged and can come somewhere with me. I can't wait to have you back home. It's boring being the only young one with these two old-timers.'

Adam punched Neil playfully. 'Less of the old, mate.'

Kate smiled, looking more like our old Kate. 'I've missed you too, bro.' She peered up at Adam and me. 'Give him yours. I can't wait to see what you've bought him.'

Adam handed Neil a large package wrapped in motorcycle gift wrapping. Neil ripped off the paper. 'New leather jacket. Thanks Mam and Dad.'

'Well, your other one was looking the worse for wear.' I passed him a carrier bag. 'And these are things to keep. You know? Mementos.'

One by one he unwrapped the items. 'A silver tankard. Cheers. Cool.' He read out the engraving. '*To Neil, Happy 18th, love Mum, Dad and Kate. 22nd October, 1972.*' The next item he tore the wrapping from was a large silver-coloured *18* key.

'Key to the door.' Kate chuckled.

'And old enough to drink legally.' Neil laughed. 'Not that it's stopped me before.'

Adam pointed a finger at him. 'Except when you're driving my baby.'

'Don't worry, Dad. I never drink and drive.'

'There are more pressies,' I said, 'keep digging.'

Some of them were joke gifts like jelly beans, marbles, a plastic pipe that you blew and made a small ball lift in the air, and a pair of wind-up teeth. Neil wound up the teeth and put them on the windowsill making us all laugh as they bobbed along chattering.

He took out the last box from the bag. 'This looks interesting.' He handled the small package, covered in 18th birthday paper before tearing off the wrapping. 'A watch. Jeez, Mam and Dad. This is so cool.' He slipped the gold-plated bracelet over his wrist.

'It does have an engraving on the back,' I said.

'Groovy.' Neil kissed me on the cheek and hugged Adam. 'Thanks, Mam, Dad, and Kate, for these beauts.' He popped the gifts back into the carrier with the exception of the wallet and watch. The watch stayed on his wrist and the wallet went inside his jeans pocket.

Adam looked at me and I nodded. He disappeared from the dayroom and in no time at all returned carrying a motorbike-shaped cake with eighteen candles alight. The nurses, patients and visitors sang, 'Happy Birthday.' I signalled to Kate and we joined in. Neil blushed. I hadn't seen him do that since primary school.

Adam put the decorated cake down in front of our son. 'I reckon you'd best make that wish quickly and get these candles blown out before they cause a fire.'

Neil laughed. 'That's easy.' He closed his eyes momentarily and blew the candles out in one breath.

Everyone clapped. One of the nurses brought over a knife.

'Cheers.' Neil positioned the knife across the cake's motorbike pillion as though he was cutting through while we all gathered around him. The nurse clicked the frame using my Kodak instamatic camera before handing it back to me.

'You'll have some cake? You and the other nurses?' I asked.

Her face radiated delight. 'Thank you. A small piece would be nice.' She tapped Neil on the shoulder. 'Happy Birthday, birthday boy. I expect you'll be celebrating in the pub this evening.'

'You bet. Thanks for taking the piccie.'

'You're welcome.' She patted his arm. 'I'd best get on.'

I whispered to Neil. 'Did you wish for something nice?'

'I did.' He smirked. 'I wished our Kate would be well and home soon. It's not the same without her.'

'That's a lovely wish.' I sliced through the sponge and passed a piece each to Neil, Adam and Kate in a white serviette.

Without being obvious I held my eyes on my daughter as she nibbled cake crumbs. She was going to get better. I blinked to stop the tears.

Chapter Thirty-Seven

Rachel

Joe rolled the ball and all of the pins went flat. The screen above the lane showed a strike. Stu was up next. He rolled a strike too. On my turn, I picked up the lightest ball, which still felt heavy, put my fingers and thumb in the correct holes, and swung my arm a couple of times before letting go.

The skittles fell. 'Yes, yes.' I jumped.

'Seven down.' Joe squeezed me. 'Well done, darling.'

'I thought I had a strike then too.'

'Never mind. We're still winning.'

Linda scooped up a ball and sent it down the lane. 'Oops.' She giggled as the ball went down the gutter. 'Sorry, Stu.'

'Last go for Joe and Stu.' I rubbed my hands.

Joe went first. A strike.

'Come on, Joe,' I cheered.

He rolled again. Another strike.

'Yay.' I clapped my hands in the air.

'It's not over till the fat lady sings.' Stu picked up the heavy ball and let it drop down the lane. A strike. He rolled again. Seven pins down. 'Only right that the birthday boy should win.' Stu shook hands with Joe. 'One of these days, Davies, I'll manage to beat you.'

Joe rubbed his chin. 'Chinny reckon.'

We left the bowling area and changed our footwear at the shoe station before making our way to the café for burger and fries. The table was dressed with balloons. Joe covered his face. 'Whose bright idea was this?'

I put a hand to my mouth. 'Guilty as charged. You do like it?'

Joe blinked. 'Of course, babe.' He blushed.

'Oh no.' I looked at Linda and Stu. 'I didn't mean to embarrass him.'

We trundled one after another into The Six Bells. I marched up to the bar. 'You lot sit down. The drinks are on me.' I pulled a note from my purse and held it out so the barmaid could see I was ready.

'Hello Rachel, how's the birthday boy?' the landlady asked.

'He's good thanks, Debs.' I leaned on the counter. 'I thought I'd get a bottle of Cava and four glasses. What do you reckon?'

'That sounds like a fabulous idea. Tell you what, it's on the house from Harry and me. If anything, to celebrate the fact that he's finally legal to serve.' She grinned.

'Do you think you could put some crisps and peanuts out too? I'll pay.' I opened my purse.

'Put your money away, kid. I'll get someone to bring over the fizz and snacks.'

'Cheers, Debs.' I made my way back to the others on our regular table by the dartboard. 'Drinks will be here in a minute. Debs and Harry are treating us.' I kissed Joe on the lips. 'And then it's pressie time.'

Within seconds Harry, the landlord, headed over to our table with a bottle of Cava in an ice bucket. 'I hear celebrations are in order. Twenty-one I hope, after I've been serving you alcohol for close on a year.'

'Yep, that's right.' Joe chuckled.

Harry poured the sparkling wine into the glasses.

⁓

Joe and I cuddled up on the back seat of the 1600E. 'Did you like your present?' I asked.

'Not half. I'd best not give up smoking though, or the lighter won't get any use. Love the inscription, *Love you forever.* I'll love you forever too.' He kissed me full on the lips. 'Of course, the best present I could have from you is this.'

⁓

News at Ten chimed from the television as I turned the key in the door. I slipped off my shoes and tiptoed upstairs, but before I had time to reach the landing, Mum was in the hallway. 'Where do you think you're creeping off to? Come on down and tell your father and me how your day's been.'

'Okay, Mum, but I need to whip to the loo first as I'm desperate.'

'Too much information, Rachel. Off you go then. I'm making Ovaltine. Would you like a cup?'

'No thanks.' I hurried up the rest of the stairs and into the bathroom. Glared at my flushed face in the mirror. Would they be able to tell what I'd been doing? I fixed my clothes in position. Not that I'd done anything wrong. After washing my face in the sink and making myself presentable I made my way back downstairs and into the kitchen where Mum was spooning the caramel coloured powder into two mugs. 'You sure you don't want one?'

'Sure, thanks.'

'Did Joe have a good birthday?'

'Yes. We went bowling.'

'Did he like his gift?' She moved over to the table and tapped a chair gesturing me to sit down before sitting down herself. 'I'd like a word.'

I took the seat next to her. 'He did thanks.' Mum and Dad had abandoned the idea of getting him a present after I'd announced our engagement. I clasped my hands wondering what she wanted to talk about. I hoped it wasn't going to be another row.

Her eyes were drawn to my finger. 'You're still wearing it then?'

I moved my hands under the table. 'Yes, of course. Look, Mum, I don't see the problem as I'm not planning to get married until I'm at least twenty-five.'

'Perhaps you could tell your father that. He's worried about you, as am I.' She rested her hand on my arm. 'Your father's got a check-up at the hospital tomorrow so no arguments.'

I smiled. 'I don't like arguing either.'

'Off you go, then. Here take this.' She handed me a mug of steaming Ovaltine before ushering me into the lounge. 'Go and see him. I'll give you a few minutes before coming in. Are you sure you wouldn't like a bedtime drink to help you rest?'

'All right then. Thanks.' I took a deep breath and headed into the lounge. 'Evening, Dad. This is for you.' I put the hot drink on the coffee table. 'Mum said you've got your check-up tomorrow.'

'Yes, I have, but hopefully it'll just be routine. Why don't you come and sit next to your old dad for a while.'

'Sure.' I sank into the comfy sofa.

'What have you been up to today? We missed you at lunchtime.' He put his arm around my shoulder.

'I went bowling with friends for Joe's birthday.'

'Oh yes, Joe' – he dropped his arm – 'the lad that's intent on spoiling my daughter's future.'

My first instinct was to shoot up from the sofa and start shouting but I remembered Mum's words, so instead I took a deep breath and said, 'He's not going to ruin my future, Dad. As I've just told Mum, Joe and I don't plan to get married for years. We both agree we're too young at the moment, but that doesn't mean we can't be committed to each other. You really upset me when you inferred I was doing things I oughtn't.'

He put his arm back around me. 'I'm sorry, love. I should never have said that. It's just...'

'What.' I looked him in the face.

'You're our little girl and I know what some of these chaps can be like. Not respecting a girl. Just like that American chap who got Peggy into trouble. And then look what happened...' He smiled. 'Mind you I've no regrets there. You were the best thing to happen to us.'

'Really?'

'Really. You've no idea how your mum and I have felt these past months when out of the blue, more than eighteen years later, the woman who gave birth to you turns up in your life.'

The television blared. I rose from the sofa to turn it off. I hadn't given any thought to how my parents felt. 'I'm sorry.' I sank back into the sofa. 'I never thought but...'

'What?'

'But you were being hard on me way before Peggy was on the scene. I was always in trouble. Arguments all the time but never with Jenny. Always me.'

Dad picked up his drink and took a sip. 'That's because you were going through a rebellious stage. It didn't mean you weren't loved.' He put his mug back down. 'We'd have been the same with Jennifer if she'd acted in that manner, or come home engaged ... Thankfully, she's not started seeing boys yet, but I'm sure once she does, we'll be in this exact same place. It's nothing to do with you being adopted. We love you just as much as your sister.' Dad smiled.

I kissed him on the cheek and cuddled up to him. 'I love you, Dad.'

He gave me a little squeeze as Mum came in with a tray and set it down on the table. 'Everything okay?'

'It is now,' Dad said, and I smiled.

She passed me a mug. 'Help yourself to a Jaffa Cake. I know they're your favourite.'

I unhooked my coat and hurried across the road to Woolies. Mr Peters had agreed Linda and I could use the staffroom as the weather had turned so cold. 'Only because you were a favourite employee of mine,' he'd said.

I pushed the shop door open, instantly hit by the warmth inside forcing me to unbutton my coat.

'Hello there, Rachel,' Mrs Davies called out as I walked by the grocery aisle.

'Hi, Mrs Davies.' I waved.

Gloria came from behind the sweet counter and hugged me. 'Hello pet, how are you? We've missed your smiling face. Here to see Linda?'

'Yep. Mr Peters has given me permission to go upstairs.'

She nudged me gently. 'Best get up there then. Linda's already there.'

'Cheers.' I made my way to the doorway to the stairs and charged up, knocking on the staffroom entrance. 'Only me.'

Linda was at the Formica table. She beamed as I entered. 'It's like old times with you being here. Wouldn't it be wonderful if you decided to come back?'

I laughed. 'It's not going to happen. I love my job. So' – I teased the greaseproof paper away from her sandwiches – 'what have we here?'

She pulled a face. 'Potted beef, I'm afraid.'

'That's okay. I love potted beef,' I lied, 'and I've got cheese and pickle so we can have one of each.' I dug into the carrier for the Tupperware container, opened it and swapped a sarnie with my friend. 'And...' I pulled out a packet of Golden Wonder cheese and onion crisps. 'These will give the paste a bit of a kick.'

Her eyes lit up. 'So?'

'So what?'

'What happened last night once you and Joe were alone?'

I shook my head. 'I'm not sure I know what you mean.' I grinned.

'You didn't?' She clapped her hands. 'You did?'

'Shut up and eat your sarnie.' I bit into one of Linda's and tried not to show my distaste. 'He's meeting my mother next week. I wonder how that will go?' I added a few crisps between the slices of bread to give it some crunch.

'I'm sure it'll be fine,' Linda said as the kettle on the stove whistled. She moved away from the table and made two coffees. 'Here. Black, just the way you like it.' She pushed a mug towards me across the table.

'Ta. I hope you're right. I'm so nervous after the reaction from Mum and Dad but there again if Peggy doesn't like him, she can lump it.'

'Exactly.' Linda rubbed her stomach. 'I'm still hungry. Got anything else?'

I chuckled. 'You mean like a packet of Jammie Dodgers?'

'You haven't?'

'I have.' I pulled them from the paper carrier. 'Help yourself.' I took one. 'Look, I'll leave the rest with you as I'd better head back to work.' I gulped back the remains of my coffee. 'See you at the weekend?'

'Sure. Mam's expecting you for Sunday lunch.'

'Ta-ra then. Have a good afternoon.'

Chapter Thirty-Eight

Peggy

Doctor Winter made her way over to us in the dayroom. 'Good afternoon, Mr and Mrs Davies. Do you mind if we have a chat in my office? Kate's brother can keep her company.'

Butterflies whirred inside me. What was she going to say? Had Kate had a setback or was it going to be good news? I became unbalanced standing up. Adam noticed and took my arm. 'It'll be all right,' he whispered.

I nodded. 'We'll be back soon,' I said to the kids before being led out of the ward on Adam's arm and guided into the doctor's office.

'Sit down, please.'

We lowered ourselves onto the soft chairs.

'Don't look so worried.' The doctor opened a file. 'It's good news.'

'It is?' I breathed out.

'Yes. Your daughter, Kate, has been doing really well. So well that I'm fairly confident that she should be able to go home next week.'

I turned to Adam. He gripped my hand. 'When?' he asked.

'Friday, unless anything changes. However, I would like Kate to continue therapy as an outpatient.'

My heart thumped. 'We'll make sure she does that.'

'And you'll need to watch for any signs of her illness resurfacing.'

'Yes. Yes.' I squeezed Adam's fingers. This was good news. A time to put our family back together.

'I'll arrange for a timetable of Kate's sessions to be printed out and given to you before her discharge.'

'May we tell Kate?' Adam asked.

'Yes. Yes, you may.'

'Thank you, Doctor.' I shook her hand. 'Thank you so much.'

I washed the last plate and placed it in the drainer. 'I don't suppose you fancy coming with me this evening?'

Adam dried up the dish. 'To be honest, Peg, I think I'd rather curl up on the couch and watch a bit of telly. These past few weeks have been exhausting and it looks like we can finally relax a bit.'

'I understand. I wonder what this Joe is like?'

'Well, you haven't got long before you find out. Don't be late back though, love. I thought we could celebrate our Kate coming home.'

'If I could cancel, I would.'

'I know.' He ruffled my hair.

'Do you mind if I take the car instead of mucking around with buses?'

'Sure. Keys are on the sideboard.'

I threw off my pinny. 'What do you think? Will I do?' I did a spin.

'You'll do.'

The Six Bells was busy and smoky when I arrived. I searched the crowd for Rachel. She spotted me first and waved me over.

'Hello,' I said on reaching her, 'Joe not arrived yet?'

'No but he shouldn't be long. You look happy?'

'Yes, I am. We had some good news about Kate today. She should be back home by next week.'

'That is great news. Would you like a drink?'

'Shall we wait until your young man arrives, and then I'll get a round in?'

'All right. He should be here in a minute.'

'I was thinking –' I tapped my fingers on the table – 'with Kate on the mend it might be the right time for you to meet your brother and sister. Would you like that?'

Rachel beamed a wide smile. 'Oh yes, I'd love that. I've been wanting to meet them for so long.' She glanced up. 'Joe's coming now.'

I turned to look. Oh my God. No, it couldn't be. 'Where?' I asked.

'The lad in the leather jacket coming our way.'

The room spun. 'No, that can't be Joe?'

Neil kissed Rachel before glaring at me. 'Mam. What are you doing here?'

'Mam? What do you mean?' Rachel asked.

'More to the point, Neil, what are you doing here?'

'Neil. No.' Rachel's face paled. 'No, this is Joe not Neil.'

Neil looked at me and then Rachel. 'How has this happened?'

'So, if she's your mam and my mother that makes you and me... Oh my God. I'm going to be sick.' Rachel picked up her coat and bag and ran from the pub.

'Rachel, wait...' Neil charged after her.

'Neil,' I called. 'Let's talk about this.'

He glimpsed back and shouted. 'I don't want to fuckin' talk. This is your fault. I hate you.'

The room went blank. I came to with a young lad shaking me. 'Are you all right, Missus. Debs, come quickly.'

Through the blur I spotted a woman heading towards me. 'Are you okay?' she asked. 'Looks like you fainted. Have you had a shock?'

I nodded.

'You'd better come through to the back and I'll make you some sweet tea.'

What just happened? Neil is Joe? Oh my God, supposing... Rachel said they hadn't had sex, they'd planned to wait, but that was months ago, back in April or May, suppose their situation had changed. I had to speak to Neil. This was not a conversation we could overlook, whether he wanted to speak to me or not. 'I have to get home.'

'You're in no fit state to go anywhere.' She put her hand around my waist. 'Lean on me.'

Before I knew it, I was sinking into an armchair in a room at the back of the pub.

'Harry,' the woman called, 'bring some sweet tea. This woman's had a shock.' She touched my face. 'You're still very white. Do you feel like you're going to faint again?'

'No. I'm all right. I need to find Neil and Rachel.'

The woman squinted. 'Neil? No Neil here, love. Do you mean Joe? Joe with Rachel? Lovely couple.' She turned to her side. 'Thanks Harry.' She turned back to me. 'Here, drink this.'

I took a sip of the drink and screwed up my face.

'I know, I know, but it'll help. Want to talk about it?'

'No, I don't, but thank you, and thank you for your kindness, but I need to be off now.'

'You mentioned your husband. Can I give him a call?'

'No. I've got the car. I'll drive home.'

'Go up to my bathroom then and swill your face. Upstairs and first on the right. You can't go anywhere like that. I'd never forgive myself if something happened to you.'

I closed the front door behind me. 'Adam. Adam.'

He came rushing to the hallway. 'Whatever's happened? Surely, he can't have been that bad.' He put his arm around me and led me into the lounge. 'Did you drive in this state?'

'Yes. I'm fine. Well, no, I'm not fine, but I was okay to drive. Oh my God, Adam.' I covered my eyes and sank into the couch.

'What on earth has happened?'

'It's Neil.'

'Neil. What's happened to Neil?'

'Neil...'

'Spit it out, woman, for God's sake tell me what's happened to my son.'

I shook my head, wiping my eyes. 'Nothing physical. It's...'

'What, Peg. What is it? You're frightening me.'

'Neil is Joe.'

'Talk sense, woman.'

'I went to meet Joe and Joe never arrived because there is no Joe. Neil is Joe. Our Neil. Rachel and Neil are engaged.'

Adam paced backwards and forwards across the room, his hand over his forehead saying, 'What a fuckin' mess. What a fuckin' mess. Are you telling me that Rachel's Joe is our son, therefore they're brother and sister?'

'Yes. Yes, that's exactly what I'm trying to say.' I sniffled.

'This is your doing. Your doing alone. If you'd done what I asked months ago they'd have found out then that they were siblings, but no... Peggy had to have her special time with her firstborn. Bloody hell, Peg.' He raised his voice. 'Well, I hope you're bloody satisfied.'

'Of course, I'm not. What a stupid thing to say. And yes, I know it's my fault.' I raised my voice, 'Don't you think I've been telling myself that. I don't need you telling me too.'

'Where's Neil now?'

I shook my head. 'I don't know. He rushed out of the pub after Rachel.'

Adam put a hand to his forehead, bending and shaking his head. 'Is he on the bike?'

'I don't know. I suppose he must be.'

'If anything's happened to him, Peg, I'll tell you now... I'll never forgive you.'

'And I'll never forgive myself,' I shouted as the front door slammed shut and heavy footsteps charged upstairs.

'Neil,' Adam called, 'we need to see you. In here now.'

Lighter footsteps came downstairs and Neil pushed the door open. 'I've nothing to say. I'm packing a bag.'

'To go where?' Adam said. 'I understand you're upset but we need to sort this out.'

'Has she told you?' Neil pointed towards me, his face contorted. 'Has she?'

'She has. Sit down for a minute. I understand how upset you must feel but there are questions to be asked and answered.'

'Like what?' Neil flopped into an armchair.

'Like for instance... this isn't something a father likes to ask his son but we need to know. How far have you and this girl gone? You know...'

Neil glared at Adam. 'My wish would be that she was pregnant.'

Adam rubbed a hand across his mouth. 'Don't be so absurd.'

I gasped, too stunned to join in with the conversation.

'I'm going to ask her to run away with me. We can still be together and get married as planned. No one else will know.'

'It's incest, lad, for fuck's sake.' Adam brushed hair away from his brow. 'You can't do that. Is she in agreement with this farcical plan?'

'She might be.'

Adam turned to me. 'Look what you've done.'

I broke down again. 'I didn't know. How could I know? She said he was Joe not Neil.'

Adam turned back to Neil. 'And you, what game were you playing, using a false name?'

'No game, I've been Joe for years. Ever since the kids at school used to call me little Joe from *Bonanza*. You know that. They thought I looked like him, and I liked it so it stuck. You know I hated that awful name Neil so I became Joe. None of my friends know me as anything other than Joe, even the tutor at college calls me Joe, so why should I have introduced myself to Rachel as anything other?'

Adam rubbed his forehead. 'What a fuckin' mess.'

Chapter Thirty-Nine

Rachel

Sobbing, I hammered my fist on the front door.

Mrs Smith part-opened it and peeped out of the crack. 'Good God, girl. You'd best come in.' She pulled the door wide. 'Take your boots off and I'll get a towel.'

'Can I go up?'

'Best not, dear, not dripping like that. I don't want my nice clean carpet messed up as I only shampooed it earlier. Keep on the mat until we get you dry. It's turned horrid out there this evening. Whatever are you doing out in it?' She yelled at the bottom of the stairs. 'Linda. Rachel's here.' She turned back to me. 'I'll get that towel.'

My friend raced downstairs. 'What the hell's happened? Aren't you supposed to be with Joe and your mother?'

I broke down again.

Mrs Smith returned with a towel and rubbed my hair. 'Take your coat off and I'll hang it up. Linda put the kettle on.'

I unbuttoned my wet coat. When I'd run out of the pub, I hadn't expected to be caught in a storm. The weather must've been in sympathy with me. When passing my dripping mac to Linda's mum, I noticed she was in her dressing gown. 'I'm sorry, you're ready for bed but...' I started sobbing again.

'Don't worry, love. It's obvious you're upset. Come into the kitchen and we'll get a hot drink inside you and you can tell us all about it' – she rested her fingers on my wrist – 'that's if you want to.'

I nodded. 'Thank you.' I followed her into the kitchen and dropped onto one of the white chairs at the table, burying my head in my hands. Linda placed her arm around me. 'Whatever's happened?'

'Joe.'

'What about Joe?' Linda squeezed my fingers.

'Get this down you.' Mrs Smith put a cup of tea in front of me. She patted my back. 'It'll help warm you up. Shall I pour one for you, Lind?'

'No, thanks, Mam. I'm okay.'

'Would you like me to leave you two girls alone?'

I reached for Mrs Smith's arm. 'Stay, please.' I sobbed into her orange quilted housecoat.

'Okay, lovey. Why not tell us what happened?'

'My mother... remember I told you I was adopted? Well, my real mother was to meet Joe...' I wiped my nose with a hanky. 'I... I just don't know how to say this. But...'

'Take your time.' Mrs Smith smiled.

'Yep, take your time.' Linda rubbed my shoulder. 'We're here for you.'

A thunderbolt made us jump and within moments a flash of lightning filled the windowpane.

'It sounds close,' Mrs Smith said, 'you shouldn't have been out in that.'

'I think someone up there is as angry as I am.'

Linda shivered. 'I hate storms. I'm glad you're here.' She perched on a chair and pulled it next to me. 'Your mother didn't like Joe then? Or one of them didn't show?'

'No, they both showed. That was the problem. The moment Joe turned up my whole world fell apart.'

Linda blinked. 'I don't understand.'

'My brother is Neil.'

'Yes, I know that' – Linda shook her head – 'but what's he got to do with it?'

'Because…' I burst out crying again. 'Because' – I blew my nose – 'because Neil is Joe or Joe is Neil, whichever way you want to put it but it still comes down to one thing that they are both the same person.' I bawled.

'Oh my God.' Linda covered her mouth with a hand. 'Oh my God. I don't know what to say. How could this have happened?'

'Indeed.' Mrs Smith joined in. 'How could this happen? Were there not any clues?'

'Well, I knew Joe had a sixteen-year-old sister in hospital and my mother had a daughter of the same age also sick. But we discussed that, didn't we, Lind?'

'Yep, we did' – she glimpsed up at her mam – 'and we concluded it was just a coincidence. After all, coincidences happen all the time, don't they?'

'Yes, I suppose they do.' Mrs Smith pulled a chair from the table and joined us. 'But what about the surname? Didn't you know Joe's?'

'Yes.' I rose from my seat and marched across the kitchen in stocking feet. 'But his name's Davies, for Pete's sake. I mean who isn't called blasted Davies around this area. There were two in my class at school, one at college, and then there's Mrs Davies at Woolies. He was Joe Davies and my brother Neil Davies. Why or how could I have connected them as the same person?'

Mrs Smith shook her head.

'You couldn't,' Linda said. 'Joe had us all fooled. Why the hell does he go around telling people he's Joe when he's not? I mean, even Stu calls him Joe, doesn't he?'

I whimpered. 'Exactly. I couldn't have known.' I sloped back to the table and sipped the warm tea.

'You should stay here tonight,' Linda said. 'That's okay, isn't it, Mam?'

'Yes, yes of course.'

'No, I can't. Mum and Dad will be worried if I don't go home.'

'It looks like the storm's passing.' Linda stood up and came over to me. 'We can run down the road to the phone box and you can call them.'

'No.' Sniffling, I wiped a hanky across my eyes. 'No, I should go home. I need to tell them what's happened and I've work in the morning.'

Mrs Smith moved closer and rubbed the top of my arm. 'Whatever you decide is all right with me but if you're not staying then you should call a taxi. You can't walk home in the dark on your own. Storm or no storm.'

As the cab driver drove off, I unlocked the front door, stepped onto the mat, pulled off my boots and hung my coat on the peg.

Mum came out into the hallway. 'Whatever's happened?'

I started sobbing again, only this time, let out the words, 'Because Joe isn't Joe.'

Dad came from the lounge. 'What's going on?'

'See if you can get some sense out of her,' Mum said. 'She appears to be talking nonsense. Have you been drinking, Rachel?'

'No.' I blubbered again.

'Come and sit down and tell us calmly what's happened.' Dad led me into the sitting room.

I sank into the sofa as rain lashed on the windowpane. A bolt of lightning made me jump. It seemed like the weather really was on my side.

Chapter Forty

Rachel

Mr Strange closed the outside door behind me. 'Goodnight, Miss Webster. We'll see you in the morning.'

I was about to cross over when someone touched my arm. 'Rach.'

'Joe' – I pushed his hand off me – 'what the hell are you playing at?'

'I need to talk. Please.'

'There's nothing left to say.' I looked across the road at my bus pulling into the stop. 'That's my bus.'

'Please, Rachel. A few minutes. You owe me that at least.'

'I owe you?' I was close to bashing him on the head with my handbag. 'Just leave me alone.'

'I will, I promise, if you hear me out first. Let's go for a coffee.'

I shook my head. There was no way he was going to give up and I suppose we should speak about what had happened. Sometime, not yet though, sometime in the future we needed to accept each other as brother and sister. 'All right. A quick coffee and then I'm going home.'

'That's all I ask.' He went to take my hand.

'No. You can't do that.'

'Sorry.'

We trekked over to the nearest café where no one knew us. Joe went up to the counter while I slumped into a chair. My heart pounded. What was the point of this? Words weren't going to change things. We might love each other but it wasn't possible. Not now. Not now we knew.

Joe made his way over with two mugs and set them down on the table. 'How are you doing?'

'How the hell do you think I'm doing?'

'I'm sorry.' He took my hand but I pulled it back. 'Although...'

'What?'

'I've nothing really to be sorry for.'

I raised my voice. 'You lied?'

'Shh,' Joe said, 'people are looking.'

I glimpsed up at the manager and nodded to let him know all was well. 'Why did you lie?' I asked in a softer tone.

'I didn't, not really. I am Joe. I've been Joe for years. I mean who the hell would want a name like Neil?'

'There's nothing wrong with the name.'

'Well, I hated it, and when the kids at school started calling me Little Joe, I liked it.'

'But why would they call you that?' I blew my nose.

'Did you ever watch *Bonanza*?'

'Sure.'

'Then don't you think I resemble Little Joe?' He smiled, acting like everything was normal.

I shrugged. 'A little I suppose but you can't just stop being one person and become someone else.'

'Why not? I did, and it's not been a problem. Did Mam tell you about Kate and me?'

'She mentioned I had a brother and sister called Neil and Kate.'

'So you had a head start on me then as I never had an inkling that there was a sister out there somewhere. How long have you known about us?'

'A while. Close on a year but I only knew about Neil and Kate. Not Joe. I'm surprised your mother never told you about me. She kept telling me it wasn't the right time to meet. Maybe if we had, we'd have been able to put a stop to this before getting so far.'

'But, Rachel' – he took my hand again – 'don't you see? It doesn't have to make a difference.'

I pulled my hand away and hid it under the table.

'We love each other. I'm Joe Davies. Your brother's Neil. We can still be together. Go away somewhere, get married. No one would know.'

'Joe.' I closed my eyes momentarily. 'Joe, I'd know. We'd know. We can't do this.'

'Please, Rach. Why not?'

'Because you're my brother and it would be wrong and because' – I stood up away from the table – 'because quite frankly, Joe, Neil, whatever your name is, it's disgusting. Now I'm going to catch my bus. Please don't come after me.'

Dad patted my arm. 'How are you doing today?'

I rubbed my eyes. 'I'll get there. I'm glad your check-up went well.' I yawned. 'I think I'll head up to bed.'

'Take it one day at a time, love.'

A motorbike engine roared outside reminding me of Joe. The next thing the doorbell chimed.

Dad glanced at me. 'Who can that be at this time?'

'I've no idea.' I went to open it but he moved me out of the way.

'Step back. I'll answer at this time of night.' He pulled the door slightly.

'Please Mr Webster can I speak to Rachel.'

I pushed my way through. 'Whatever are you doing here? I told you earlier.'

'I know but...'

He didn't get any further before Dad cut in, 'Look lad, I know you've had a shock too but you have to respect Rachel's wishes. She's told you that she doesn't want to see you. In time you may both be able to get over this and get to know each other as brother and sister but for now, I suggest you be on your way.'

'But Mr Webster, please. Please, I need to see Rachel. I just need to talk.'

'Sorry, lad.' Dad closed the door on Joe. 'Get yourself to bed, love. He'll get over it.'

'Thanks, Dad.' I trudged upstairs to my bedroom and threw myself onto my bed and sobbed. Joe may get over it, but would I?

Chapter Forty-One

Peggy

Adam held out the handpiece. 'It's for you.'

'Hello.' I smiled as he hovered over me.

'Yes, okay. I'll be there.' I returned the receiver to its cradle. 'It was Rachel.'

'I know that but what did she want?'

'She wants to meet up with me later today.'

'Oh?'

'Well, I am still her mother. That hasn't changed.'

'Just tread carefully. We've got our Kate home in three days and I don't want her walking back into a firing line. She needs a peaceful family atmosphere.'

'I know. Don't worry. You could always come with me.'

'No. I don't want to be involved. Once things have settled down and Neil's happy about accepting Rachel as his sister, then... and only then, you can bring her home to meet Kate. Until then I don't want our Kate knowing anything about her. Is that understood, Peg?'

'Loud and clear.'

After parking the car, I made my way to The Three Horseshoes where neither of us were known.

Rachel was shivering in the entrance. 'Thanks for meeting me,' she said but the normal kiss on the cheek was absent.

'Well of course I'd meet you. Nothing's changed between you and me.'

She shook her head. 'Nothing's changed? You must be joking. Let's go inside because it's too cold out here.'

I followed her through the door and up to the bar. 'What would you like?' I asked.

'Just a Coke.' She headed over to a table at the back of the pub.

'Two Coca-Colas,' I said to the barmaid. Rachel had asked to see me yet appeared cold. What was going on? I felt nauseous at what had happened to my family. Poor Neil was a right mess but at least Adam had convinced him not to move out, and like Adam had said, we needed to create a calm atmosphere for Kate's homecoming. It should have been a happy time but with all this...

The barmaid flicked the lids off the bottles and put them on the counter in front of me along with two glasses. I passed her a fiver and she handed back my change. I poured the Cokes into the tumblers and carried them over to Rachel.

'Ta.' She picked up the drink and took a sip. She bit her lip. 'I'm not sure how to say this but...'

'What?'

'You've got to keep Joe, I mean Neil, away from me. He keeps pestering me.'

'He's what?'

'Pestering me. Came to the newspaper office yesterday after I'd finished work. I agreed to go for a coffee to get him off my back but then he turned up outside my house last night at eleven o'clock. Apart from not being fair on me, it's not fair on my parents either. My dad had been to the hospital yesterday...'

'Is he okay?'

'Yes, but that's not the point. He may well have not been. It isn't fair. I don't like this anymore than Joe does but I'm not about to continue a romantic relationship with my brother.'

I brushed her fingers. 'Of course not. No one would expect that.'

She pulled her hand away. 'You're wrong. He does. Neil. Joe. Whoever he is. He's got his head in the clouds and thinks we can still make a go of it. Move somewhere and get married.'

I put my hand over my mouth to stop myself from gagging. Why would Neil be doing this? Surely, he could see how wrong it was. 'I'll speak to Adam and we'll talk to Neil together. We can't afford arguments in the house right now with Kate's homecoming and I'm afraid...'

'What are you saying?'

'Adam said I need to forget about bringing you home until time has lapsed and you and Neil can look at each other differently.'

I took a gulp of my drink. 'I completely agree with Adam. It's your son you need to convince. Oh, and I'm thinking of asking work for some leave and taking Mike up on his offer of those airline tickets. You can come with me if you like?'

'I'm not sure, Rachel. I'll discuss it with Adam.'

She forced a smile. 'Whatever. Just keep Joe off my back.' She emptied her glass. 'I need to get home now as Mum will have my dinner ready.'

'I can give you a lift?'

'No, best not. If Mum and Dad clapped eyes on you right now, I think they may well lose it.'

'All right. I'm sorry. This should never have happened.'

'No, it shouldn't have. Joe and I had something really special and now that's gone. I'm left empty, as he is too, but Joe's deluded if he really thinks we can live together as husband and wife. I've got to go.' She fastened her coat and left me sitting at the table.

'Well? What did she want?' Adam was almost in my face.

'For me to keep Neil away. Apparently, he's been turning up at her workplace and at her home pestering her to run away with him.'

Adam ran his fingers through his hair. 'Fuck, he's not still going on about that. That's what he was saying Sunday evening. I thought he'd calmed down and come to his senses. We need to talk to him. He should be home in a minute.'

I switched the oven on and stuck in the cottage pie I'd made earlier. Not that I had any appetite but we had to try and eat. This should have been a happy time with Kate being discharged but all I could feel was dread. Supposing she picked up on what was going on, would that cause her to go backwards? Like Adam said, we needed to ensure she came home to tranquil surroundings.

The front door closed and Neil wandered into the kitchen. 'Hi, Dad.' He totally blanked me.

'Dinner will be ready shortly,' I said.

He continued to ignore me.

'Neil,' Adam said, 'your mam's speaking to you.'

'I've nothing to say to her.'

'Look, lad, I know how awful this is for you but we need to think about your sister. She'll be home in three days and if she comes home to this' – he took a deep breath – 'she'll be back in hospital before the weekend is out. 'We've got to move past this...'

'I can't. I'm sorry, Dad, but perhaps it's best if I move out. I'll get a flat.'

'And pay for it with what?'

'I'll go back to Elmo's. What with two jobs, even if the apprenticeship pays peanuts, maybe I'll just about be able to afford a bedsit.'

'Sit down, son.' Adam patted Neil on the shoulder.

Grudgingly Neil took a seat and leaned his elbow on the table.

'Tough as it might be for you, Kate has to come first right now. You understand that, don't you?'

He nodded. 'Of course I don't want our Kate to have a setback but...'

Adam lit up a Players. 'Want one?' He passed it to Neil who took a drag. Adam took another cigarette from the packet for himself. 'For starters, you quit Elmo's because you found it too much once you started full-time at the garage.'

'Yes but...'

'Neil, son, moving out won't fix things. Look' – Adam rested his hand on Neil's shoulder – 'you've got to stop pestering Rachel. If you're not careful she'll report you to the police. It's hard for her too and you're not helping her move past the situation.'

'But if it hadn't been for her' – he scowled at me – 'this could've been prevented. Why didn't she tell us that we had a sister somewhere?'

'I know, lad. I know. But what's done is done.' Adam flicked ash into the ashtray. 'I know it's not easy for you but promise you'll try.'

'I promise.'

'And before you think about contacting Rachel again come and talk to me.'

'Right.'

'Good.' Adam patted Neil on the back and strode out of the kitchen.

I took a seat next to Neil. 'I'm sorry. Really, I am.'

He glared at me, rose from the table, and stormed out shaking his head saying, 'Unbelievable.'

⸙

Adam stuck a forkful of cottage pie into his mouth. 'That went well then?'

'He's never going to forgive me.'

'Can you blame him? He'll have to get past this not eating with you before Kate comes home though.'

'I've been thinking about that.' I chewed some mash and carrot.

'You have a solution?'

'Possibly. Rachel's asked if I'll go away with her.'

'You mean to him, and the States?'

'Yes. It'll put some space between us.'

'And your daughter, Kate? Or have you forgotten about her?'

'No, of course not. I'm doing this for Kate to make sure there's no friction in the household.'

Adam slammed his cutlery down and pushed his plate away. 'What the hell has happened to the woman I married?'

'What do you mean?'

'For God's sake, Peg, are you really that naïve?'

'I don't understand.'

'Your son is in pieces, your daughter has a condition with complications that can kill her, yet here you are, as calm as anything, suggesting you go off to the States with your ...' He shook his head. 'You're needed here, woman. Now listen up carefully because I'm only going to say this once.'

Shaking, I stared at this man I didn't recognise.

'If you get on that plane or anywhere else for that matter with your... whatever she is. Then that's the end of us. And the end of you as mam to Neil and Kate. You'll be dead to us all. Do I make myself clear?'

My stomach churned. 'Yes. But... You can't do that.'

'Can't I? Get on that plane and try me.'

<hr />

The oven was throwing out gorgeous aromas. I looked up at the clock. Half past two. Sheila should be here by now. I headed into the lounge and peered out of the window. A maroon Ford Anglia pulled up and my sister stepped from the car. She waved to Malc as he drove off before ambling up the footpath. I went to the front door, opened it and kissed her on the cheek. 'Thanks for coming, Sheila.'

'You're welcome. Like I said on the phone though, I can't stay long, but you sounded desperate.'

'Just a bit. Come in.' I closed the door behind her. 'I've made some cookies to have with a cup of tea.'

'I can smell them.' She made her way into the kitchen and took a seat at the table. 'How's Kate doing?'

'Well, really well. She's due home in a couple of days.' I tipped water into the teapot and placed that, along with two cups and saucers, onto the table. 'I'll just get the biscuits out and then I'll tell you all about it.' I took the baking tray from the oven and slid the coconut cookies onto a plate. 'They'll be too hot at first but should cool down quickly.'

'Mmm, yum. They smell lovely. Shall I be Mum?'

'If you like.' I untied my pinny and hung it on the hook while Sheila poured tea and milk into the cups.

'Out with it then,' she said.

I helped myself to a cookie. 'These are ready to eat.' I passed her the plate. 'Hmm, this is a little delicate. You know I've been seeing Rachel?' I nibbled on a biscuit.

'Yes. How's it going? I've been wondering when you were going to get around to bringing her to mine so I can meet her properly.'

'To be honest I wanted some time for the two of us to get to know each other properly before introducing her to anyone else, but unfortunately that's blown up in my face.'

'You're not making much sense.' Sheila picked up a cookie and took a bite. 'Mmm. You haven't lost your touch in making these. Mine never come out like this. I tell you what, if you're wondering what to get me for Crimbo, make me up a box of these.'

'Sure.' I took a sip of tea. 'Right, I'll start from the beginning. Rachel and I have been meeting on a regular basis and it was going really well. We even managed to trace Mike, her father, the American guy that Dad warned off. Remember the airmail letter in the bureau? Well Mike came over in June. A bit of a plonker by all accounts. Anyway, I'm moving away from the subject. During our meet-ups Rachel chatted a lot about her young man, Joe, and last Sunday I had the chance to meet him only...'

'What?'

'Joe turned out to be our Neil.'

Sheila dropped crumbs on the floor. 'Bloody hell, how did that happen? No wonder you're in a state. How's my poor nephew?'

'In a bad way. And as to how it happened' – I scratched my nose – 'how was I supposed to connect Joe to Neil?'

She wrinkled her nose. 'Well, I suppose you wouldn't, although...'

'What?'

'Maybe something might have clicked when she mentioned his name was Joe? Even as a coincidence.'

'What?' I squinted.

'Neil, he's been calling himself Joe for years. You must've known.'

I shook my head. 'No, I had no idea.'

'Hmm, perhaps if you'd shared more about your goings on with Rachel then maybe this could've been prevented. If, for instance, you'd mentioned Joe to me, then right away, I'd have said how funny.'

'Well, I'm glad my son was able to share his fake name with you all these years but couldn't be bothered to tell his own mam.'

'I suppose because you used to get cross with him as a young boy when he told you he hated his name. "That's the name you were given at birth so get over it." Can you deny it?'

'Did I really say that?'

'You were always going on at the lad. No wonder he didn't bother telling you, but he told me. In fact, every birthday card I've had from him since he was eleven was signed as Joe. To be honest, I only ever call him Neil in your presence.'

'Thanks for that. You've now made me feel a hundred per cent worse. But...'

She crunched on a cookie. 'These really are gorgeous. You've surpassed yourself this time. Sorry, what were you saying?'

'Since Sunday evening – that's when everything blew up – Neil's been hounding Rachel. Waiting outside her work place. Turning up at her house. Goodness knows what he'll do next, although Adam's told him to stay away but... Poor Rachel can't cope. She's trying to move past this while Neil has got it into his head that they can still be a couple, disappear somewhere and get married.'

'What?'

'I know. We've warned him it's ludicrous and Rachel has said she's not interested. Even told him the thought of them together disgusts her but he still won't let it lie.' I rested my hands on the table. 'The poor lad loves her and has convinced himself it's the right thing, even though deep down he must know how wrong it is.'

'So, you'd like me to speak to him?'

'No, that's not it, although I don't suppose it would hurt. I wanted your advice. Rachel has to get away for a while and Mike's offered to send over the cash to buy plane tickets and she's asked me to go with her.'

'You're not contemplating it?'

I ran my tongue across my lip. 'Why not?'

'Because... What does Adam say?'

'This is it. Adam's turned around and said if I go, then there's no coming back. That I'll be dead to him and the kids. I'm not sure how he thinks he'll get away with that. What do you think?'

'Honestly, Peg' – she shook her head – 'I don't know how you can ask me that. I'm totally with Adam. For God's sake you've known Rachel for five minutes. What about your own kids?'

'Rachel is my own.'

'I mean the kids you've nurtured from babies. Yes, you gave birth to Rachel but after that you didn't know anything about her until she came looking for you. But your kids... They need you.'

'So, you don't think I should go?'

'Bloody right, I don't. What about your poor Kate? Struggling with an eating disorder. I told you about that girl I went to school with. And then there's poor Neil. Imagine how he's feeling now. Mixed up. Talking nonsense, yes, but that's because he's hurting and looking for answers. He needs his mam.'

'But he doesn't want me. And we need a calm household for when Kate comes home, otherwise, she could end up back in hospital. I'm doing this for Kate.'

Sheila shot up from the chair. 'My God, you really think that? Wake up, Peg, otherwise you're going to lose your whole family. Tell Rachel you can't go with her because your family needs you. She has a mam and dad, let them take care of her, and you take care of your own, and your husband. I can't imagine what this has done to Adam.'

'Thanks for that.'

'You know me, Peg, I don't beat around the bush. I tell it as it is. And you, lady, need to wake up to the right thing to do. Speak to Neil. Let him know you understand it's going to take him time to forgive you but you'll be there when he's ready, and ask him to think about Kate coming home and returning to a happy household.' Sheila picked up her bag. 'If that's it, I'd best be off. Malc will be back in a minute. Perhaps if it's okay with you, we can pop up on Sunday to see Kate?'

'Yes, sure. Why not come for tea? I'll make more cookies.'

A car tooted outside. Sheila peered out of the window. 'That's Malc back. Sorry I have to rush off, and sorry if what I said hurt but hopefully it has brought you to your senses.'

'Yes, yes, it has. Thanks for being so blunt. I'll let Rachel know I can't go with her.'

Chapter Forty-Two

Rachel

'You can come in now, Miss Webster.' Mr Strange held his office door open. 'Take a seat.'

'Thank you.' I sank into the executive chair.

'What appears to be the problem?' he asked sitting down at the opposite side of the desk.

I took a deep breath. 'I was wondering if you'd grant me some leave.'

'Now, Miss Webster, you know booking holidays should be done through Mrs Jones.' He lit up a cigar making me almost gag from the smell.

'This is the thing, Mr Strange, I need a little more than a normal holiday. Due to personal circumstances, I find myself requiring to get away for a while. As much as a month...'

'A month?'

'Yes, I'm sorry. Hopefully it won't be longer than that but... I really don't want to lose my job but I can't...' I broke down in tears.

Mr Strange picked up the phone handpiece and dialled. 'Mrs Jones, can you come in here please?' He replaced the receiver and poured a glass of water. 'Drink this.'

'Thank you.' I sobbed.

Betty rushed in. 'Yes, sir?'

'Miss Webster needs a bit of consoling and as you know I'm not good at that sort of thing. Can you look after her please? And find out exactly what it is she wants.'

'Yes, sir.'

'I'll leave you in good hands, Miss Webster. Explain the situation to Mrs Jones and we'll see what we can work out.'

'Thank you. Thank you, sir,' I answered in-between sobs.

Jenny passed me the jug of custard. I pushed it away. 'Sorry, but I can't face it.'

Mum pursed her lips. 'But you barely touched your hotpot. You must eat something.'

'I can't. Not now. If I eat, I think I'll be sick. Anyway, I've something to tell you, and I'm not sure how you're going to take it.'

'Oh?' Dad spooned a chunk of apple pie into his mouth.

'I spoke to my boss today about granting me some leave and he's agreed I can take a month's unpaid holiday starting from the twentieth of November. My plan is to go to America.'

'What?' Dad put his spoon down.

'Mike said he'll wire some cash over for plane tickets and I've asked Peggy to come with me.'

Mum frowned. 'You've done what?'

'Asked Peggy to come with me. What's wrong with that?'

'How can you ask that?'

'You know I have to get away from here. I need to put distance between me and Joe. Surely you must see that?'

'Yes, absolutely. I agree but...'

Dad took his glasses off and held them in his hand. 'You must see where your mother's coming from?'

'Quite frankly, no. Is it because I'm going to the States?'

'No.' Mum reached across the table to hold my hand. 'It's Peggy that's the problem.'

'But I thought we'd got past that. Like I've told you both over and over again, you're my mum and dad. She's just Peggy.'

Mum shook her head. 'That's not what I mean and I don't understand why you can't see what's right in front of you.'

'Well obviously I can't. Perhaps you should enlighten me.'

Mum sighed. 'Joe is as devastated as you. More so by the sounds of it. He had no idea of your existence whereas at least you knew you had a brother and another sister out there.'

'Right?' I licked my lips.

'Joe will need his mother and if she goes gadding about to the States with you... Where does that leave Joe and his sister?'

'I hadn't thought of it that way, but I don't want to go on my own. To be honest I'm scared stiff at the thought of flying.'

Mum came behind me and put an arm around my shoulder. 'You don't have to go on your own. I'll come with you. To America or wherever else you might like. Your father has work, and Jennifer has college, but apart from Women's Institute, which I can cancel, I'm free.'

I thought about the idea of Mum meeting Mike. It wouldn't work. I shook my head. 'I'm not sure.'

'If you don't want me to come with you then take a friend. Money isn't an issue. Your dad and I will pay for the tickets. You don't need anything from that Mike.'

'No, Mum, I want him to pay. He should pay. After all, it's only right that he does something for me. But who can I ask to go with me?' I drummed my fingertips on the table. 'There is one person but...'

'Linda Smith?' Mum asked.

I nodded.

'Then ask her.'

'You don't mind?'

'We just want you to be happy. Isn't that right, Charles?'

'That's right. And like your mum says, we understand you want to get away for a while but to take a mother from children who need her isn't the way. By all means see if this girl wishes to go with you. Make the arrangements and I'll drive you to Heathrow myself.'

I almost fell off the chair. I got up and hugged Mum and then Dad. 'Thank you. You're the best parents in the world.'

⊰⊱

Linda stood by Mr Peters as he locked up the shop. 'Good evening, Miss Webster,' he said, 'nice to see you again.'

'Thank you, Mr Peters.'

'Bright and early in the morning, Miss Smith.' Mr Peters ambled down the road swinging his large umbrella.

'What are you doing here?' Linda asked.

I linked my arm in hers. 'I've got something to ask you. Time for a coffee?'

'Always.'

We headed over to Elmo's. My mind slipped back to the first time I'd met Joe in here. It had been immediate love on both sides. I sniffed back the tears. It was time to look forward not dwell on what might have been.

Linda gazed at me. 'Maybe we shouldn't have come in here?'

I dabbed a hanky across my eyes. 'I have to get over it.'

A female waitress approached us. 'What would you like to order?'

I looked up at the blonde curly haired teen. 'Just two coffees.'

'I know you. Aren't you Joe's girlfriend?'

I burst out crying.

Linda stepped in. 'Not any more. They've split up but... Just bring the drinks, will you?'

'So, you'll come?' I drank back the remainder of my coffee.

'If I can sort everything. Yep. Mam won't have a problem so it just depends whether Mr Peters can manage without me for a month and at such short notice.'

'I'm sure someone can step up as temporary supervisor. Mr Strange is employing a temp for my job while I'm away. It's very good of him to keep my position open when I've not been there that long.'

'But what about your mam and dad? How are they going to take it?'

'They've already agreed.' I smiled.

'Looks like we're off to the States then, kiddo. Although, that only gives us a couple of weeks. Is that going to be enough time?'

'I don't see why not. It's just the case of booking the tickets and adding Mike's address for where we'll be staying. I believe he has a swimming pool in his garden.'

'Wow. Better pack my bikini. We can do this but...'

'What?'

'I don't have a suitcase. Oh dear, I'm not sure I'll have enough money to buy one once I pay Mam my board and keep some for spends. I wonder if Mam will help me?'

'No need for her to do that. We've got plenty of suitcases. You can borrow one of ours.'

'Your folks won't mind?'

'Nah, course not. And I'm sure Mike will treat us to plenty of stuff over there so we won't need much cash.'

'Cool.' Linda checked the time on the watch I'd bought her as a late birthday present. 'I should get home otherwise Mam's going to wonder where I am. Your bus is due shortly, isn't it?'

'Yes, thanks. I can't believe we're finally going away, and on a plane.'

***

'What have you got in there?' Mel asked as I was bundling out of work the next day armed with packed carrier bags.

'Holiday stuff. Bikinis, new frocks, sunglasses. You name it I've probably got it. Not all for me though. Linda couldn't get any extra time off work so I had to do her shopping too.'

'You must be raking the money in.'

'Not really, Mike sent over extra cash for us.'

'Lucky you.' She peered across the road. 'Isn't that Joe?'

'Oh God.' My heart hammered. 'I don't think I can cope with this. He keeps pestering me.'

'Would you like me to come over with you?'

'Nope, you get off. I'll tell him once and for all to leave me alone. Trouble is, it screws me up every time I see him, when I think of what could've been.'

Mel put her arm around me. 'I understand. You know where I am if you ever need an ear.'

'Thanks.' I wandered across to the bus stop. 'What are you doing here, Joe?'

'Please, Rachel, please can we talk? Stu said you're off to the States. I can't bear the idea of you flying off to another country and leaving us like this.'

'Joe' – I placed the heavy bags down on the bench in the shelter – 'don't you see that you're making it more painful for us both?'

'Just give me a bit of time. Don't let us end like this.'

The green double-decker pulled up. 'I'm getting on this.' I picked up the bags and climbed onto the platform without looking back.

A couple of days later I met Peggy during my lunch break at Sweet Leaf Café. When I arrived she was seated at a table with a glass of water. 'Thanks for meeting me,' she said as I reached her.

'I'd planned to call you, anyway, but I've been so busy. Is it waitress service or do I go to the counter?'

'No, she'll come here.' She took my hand. 'I hope you're not going to be cross with me but I can't...'

'What?'

'I'm really sorry but I can't come to America with you.' She blinked rapidly.

'It's all right. I understand.'

'You do?'

A plump woman with snowy hair waddled towards us. 'What can I get you ladies?'

'Just a pot of tea for two please.' Peggy smiled.

'Be a couple of minutes.' The waitress toddled off.

'You do?' Peggy repeated.

'Yes, I do.' I squeezed her hand. 'At first, I didn't, but my mum made me see things clearly. You should be at home for Neil and Kate. They need you.'

Peggy breathed a sigh of relief and smiled. 'Thank you. Adam said we'd be finished if I went with you. And that I'd be dead to the kids. I can't have that. I love you, Rachel, but I can't lose my family.' She cried into a handkerchief.

I slid into the chair next to her and put my arm around her. 'I said, I understand. It was wrong of me to ask.'

'Will you still go?'

'Yes, we're flying from Heathrow in a couple of weeks.' I dropped my arm.

'We?'

'Linda's coming with me.'

'And your parents don't mind?'

'No. They just want me to be happy.'

'They sound like good people.'

'They're the best. The plan is to go for a month. I've managed to get leave from work. Hopefully in that time I can try and put all this behind me, and Joe, I mean Neil, can too.'

'Will you speak to him before you go?'

'No. And you've reminded me why I was planning to ring you. He's still pestering me. He was outside my work again the other night.'

'He just wants to clear the air. Can you not give him half an hour to do that? I'm sure it will help you too.'

'No, and I don't know how you can ask me.'

'I had to ask.'

'Who knows, maybe I'll feel differently when I get back? I'd like to see you then, and maybe, Kate?'

'I hope you can meet Kate in time but definitely you and me will get together. Let me know the details of your flight and I'll ask Adam if we can come and wave you off. That's if you don't mind?'

'That would be nice.'

'Thank you for being so understanding. You have a kind nature.'

'Must get it from my mum.' I smiled. 'My adopted mum, I mean. Your job is to be there for Joe and Kate, sorry I can't get it into my head to call him Neil. You need to put your family back together. It's become a disaster since I arrived on the scene.'

Chapter Forty-Three

Peggy

Adam switched off the television. 'We need to talk.'

'Oh. What about?' I plumped up the scatter cushions on the settee. 'Kate appears to be doing well. She ate at least half of her dinner this evening.'

'Not about Kate but Neil.'

'He's still not speaking to me, unless Kate's around, and then at least he's acting like everything's normal.'

'Like I said, give him time. The thing is Peg, he needs closure. You need to make Rachel realise that they both do. She can't go flying off to America leaving things as they are.'

'I've tried but she just tells me to keep him away from her.'

'Then you need to try a different tactic.' Adam lit up a cigarette and passed me the packet of Players. 'Want one?'

'No, ta. So, what are you suggesting?'

'Speak to her mam. See if she can make Rachel understand how important it is.'

I'd never met her adopted mother. Would she even see me? But if I gave an outright *no* to Adam then that would cause more problems.

'Did you hear what I said?'

'I did. I'm just not sure I can face her, and she may not even see me.'

'You must try for our son. He needs this.'

'All right, I'll try. I'll phone her in the morning.'

'Good.' He yawned. 'I'm off to bed. You coming?' He stood up from the armchair.

'In a minute. I'll just clear up a bit.'

'Leave it until the morning.'

⚓

I parked the Cortina outside Rachel's house or should I say mansion. Thankfully Adam had got a lift into work so I could use the car, rather than having to catch two buses in this sleet.

As I headed through the metal gate the immaculate front garden caught my breath with its amazing colour. Purple and orange winter pansies in a bed under the window and shrubs with bright yellow flowers down the side of the drive. Flowers I didn't recognise had crimson and blue blooms. I thought of our tiny bare garden in comparison as I walked up the footpath to the detached building which our house would probably fit inside at least six times.

With my umbrella protecting my hair, hesitantly I knocked on the brass door knocker and waited. In seconds the door was opened by a plump woman wearing a smock apron, and a scarf wrapped around her head like a turban. 'Hello,' she said, 'you must be Mrs Davies? Mrs Webster is expecting you. Do come in.'

'Thank you.' I collapsed the brolly and shook it out before stepping onto the mat and wiping my feet. 'Shall I take my shoes off?'

'No need. Let me have your coat and you can pop your brolly in there.' She pointed to a stand.

I slipped off my rain mac and passed it to the woman.

'This way.' She led me into a huge sitting room where an elegant blonde-haired woman stood by a roaring fire. Suddenly I felt rather frumpy in my old tweed suit.

'Do come in, Mrs Davies,' she said. 'Donna, can you bring in some tea, please?'

'Yes, Mrs Webster.'

'My cleaner,' Rachel's mam said to me, 'she's a godsend.'

I nodded, taking in the vast wall space covered in burgundy floral paper. Large pictures with landscape country and coastal scenes hung in gilt frames around the room.

'Do sit down, please.' Mrs Webster led me to the antique chaise longue and took a seat next to me.

'Thank you.' I sank into the royal blue, deep velvet cushions. My legs trembled as I faced the older woman who'd raised my firstborn. 'And thank you for seeing me.'

'I'm intrigued although I must say it's nice to finally put a face to the name.'

'Rachel appears to be coping well.'

'She is, but more importantly how's that boy of yours? Is he still struggling to accept the situation? Rachel mentioned he's been lurking around her workplace, and he turned up here late one evening.'

'I'm sorry about that.'

'Ah, here's tea. Thank you, Donna, just pop it down and get yourself off home. I'll see you in a couple of days.'

The cleaner placed the tray down on the oval glass coffee table. 'Your coat's hanging by the front door,' she said to me before leaving.

'Earl Grey fine for you?' Rachel's mum smiled.

'Yes, thank you, Mrs Webster.'

'Rosalind, please. And may I call you Peggy?'

'Yes, thank you,' I answered, admiring the bone china teapot.

'Would you prefer milk or a slice of lemon?'

'Milk please.'

Mrs Webster poured tea from the pot, added milk into mine, and a slice of lemon into hers. She passed me the matching cup and saucer. 'Do help yourself to a biscuit.' She picked up a digestive from the plate.

'Thank you.' I didn't think I'd keep anything down right now. Mrs Webster was being polite but I still felt uncomfortable.

'About Joe. Neil,' she said once her mouth was empty.

I chewed on my lip waiting.

'It can't continue.'

I took a sip of the tea trying to keep myself calm. 'Sorry?'

'This pestering. It has to stop.'

Remembering Adam's words from the night before I took a deep breath. 'My visit here is about Neil. You're right, Mrs... Rosalind, he's struggling. He needs closure and I believe Rachel does too. Neil's desperate for a chance to sit down and talk to her. Not to put any pressure on her, as he realises now that there's no future for them, not like that. But they're brother and sister and they both need to come to terms with that.'

Mrs Webster stirred her tea. She frowned. 'Forgive me, Peggy, but I'm not quite clear what you're getting at.'

'It's a big ask, I know, but I'd like you to persuade Rachel to meet with Neil and hear him out before she goes away. Please? My son needs this.'

Holding the cup handle with her index finger and thumb she shook her head. 'I'm not sure that's a good idea. Surely, isn't that just prolonging the pain?'

'Possibly, but Neil, and I believe Rachel, should do this. Please will you help me?'

'I will consider it.'

'Thank you.' I sipped the tea trying not to screw up my nose at the taste. Give me my pot of Tetley any day.

'How is your daughter? I understand she's been quite poorly?'

'She's doing well.' I took a malted milk from the plate.

'Is she still in hospital?'

'No, she was discharged recently. She's in school today.' I took particular care not to divulge what had been wrong. 'Kate doesn't know about Rachel yet and now with...'

'I understand. Better to leave it for now.' Mrs Webster poured herself another cup of tea. 'Would you like a refill?'

'No thank you.' Head on, I confronted the elephant in the room. 'I'm sorry I brought all this into your lives. You know it was Rachel who came looking for me?'

'Yes. We know. I shan't lie, I thought it was a bad idea, but if she hadn't then she and Joe would still be together and they'd never have known they were related.'

'Hmm, yes. I hadn't thought of it that way.' I looked at Mrs Webster. 'I saw him, you know, your husband, when he came to the mother and baby home.'

She squinted. 'Sorry, you saw him when?'

'After Rachel was born.'

'I hadn't realised. Did you speak to him?'

'No. It was through a part-opened door. I heard someone call him Mr Webster when he was handed a baby. At the time though, I didn't know it was my baby. I didn't want to give her up, you know?'

'You didn't? That's rather strange as we were told the young girl had agreed to have her child adopted.'

'But that wasn't true. I hadn't agreed. My dad must've forged my signature. Or they allowed his signature because I was a minor. I didn't want to give up my baby.' Tears filled my eyes.

'I'm sorry,' Mrs Webster said, 'we didn't know.'

My mind flitted back to that day. My baby being rushed from the room the moment she was born. The nurses ignoring me when I begged them to let me hold her. And if I hadn't heard that nurse say *her*, I'd never have known all these years whether I'd given birth to a boy or girl. I dabbed my eyes.

Mrs Webster surprised me by taking my hand. 'Peggy, we didn't know.'

'I know.' I sniffed, gazing around at the rich quality furniture. 'But at least now I can see it was the right decision. She has a good home and a caring mam and dad. That's all I could wish for.'

'Listen, Peggy, I'll speak to Rachel about seeing Neil.' She sighed. 'But you know I can't promise anything.'

'Yes, I understand.'

'However, if Rachel grants a meeting, afterwards I expect you to ensure your son does not continue to bother her. Are we in agreement?'

'Yes, we are.' I rose from the comfortable chaise longue. 'Thank you for seeing me.'

Chapter Forty-Four

Rachel

When I came out of work Joe was leaning by a lamppost. 'Thank you for agreeing to meet me,' he said and gave me that gorgeous smile.

'That's okay. You're right, we do need to clear the air. It's not fair if I get on a plane and fly across the world without us having a chance to put everything behind us.'

'I've got Dad's car.' His shoulder length hair blew across his face. 'Why don't we go for a drive and I can park up somewhere to give us some privacy to talk?'

'Sure. It's too blustery to hang around here.'

He went to take my hand but must've thought better about it because he stuck his hands into his coat pockets. 'It's parked just over there.'

Pulling my Afghan coat closer to me, I followed him across to the car park, and climbed into the 1600E. He drove about half a mile down a country lane before stopping in a woodland area. 'Here do?'

'Yep. Fine.' I peered out of the window at the branches rocking as wind howled through the trees. 'So long as these don't decide to fall on us.'

'Nah. They won't do that. Look, I brought us drinks and snacks.' He pulled a khaki rucksack from the back seat and unpacked a flask and a packet of Jaffa Cakes. 'Coffee?'

'Thanks.' I smiled remembering how thoughtful he was.

He poured the drink into the beakers and passed one to me. 'That'll warm you up, and help yourself to your favourites.'

'Thanks, Joe.' The hot liquid was welcoming and my tummy gurgled at the Jaffa Cakes.

'Thank you for agreeing to this,' he said again. 'It's more than I deserve after the way I behaved.'

'It wasn't your fault. A total shock for us both. Our whole worlds blown apart.'

'Fingers crossed this trip helps you. America will be amazing. I always hoped it would be me and you going together.'

'Me, too, Joe. But we can't change what's happened.'

'No. I hate Mam for this.'

'Please don't blame Peggy. It's not her fault. She's hurting almost as much as us.'

'But if she'd...'

'She can't have known. Maybe we were drawn to each other because we're brother and sister. The same genes and all that.'

'Maybe. I remember that first day you came into Elmo's when I was on shift.'

'Me too.'

'There was something there. We instantly clicked.'

'Yep. Hopefully one day we'll both fall in love with someone else.'

'I doubt there's anyone else like you out there. It's going to take time to think of you as my sister. You were the best thing to happen to me.'

'And you for me. But we might meet someone new. Look at Peggy. She was madly in love with Mike, my father, and then after her world fell to bits, she met your dad. Adam's a much better catch than Mike. Mike's a bit of a tool.'

'Yet you're going to spend time with him?'

'Only because I have to get away. I'm hoping as Peggy won't be around, he'll concentrate on getting to know me. I don't hold out much hope though. You know he wanted your mam back and she told him where to go?'

He tucked his hair behind his ear. 'Well, no, because she never told me anything. I hate her for that,' he repeated.

'Please don't hate her. She loves you, and your sister. She's very proud of you both. Speaking about Kate. How is she?'

'She's trying.'

'Trying?' I squinted.

'You know what's wrong with her?'

'No. Peggy never said. And you never told me what was wrong with your sister.'

'All a bit tricky. She has an eating disorder but we're hoping she's on the mend. She's eating a bit now at least.'

'That's good. Will you do something for me?'

'Anything, Rach, you know that.'

I stroked his fingers. 'I want you to make peace with Peggy. Help her put your family back together again. I feel so guilty.' I dabbed my eyes with a hanky. 'Yours was a happy family before I came along.'

'But that's not your fault.'

'No, but it feels like it. Peggy's a fraction of the woman I first met. And that must be my fault. She and your dad were happy and look at them now, so please, be there for your mam and dad.'

'I'll try. No wonder I fell in love with you.' He took me into a hug. I was content, warm and safe. When his lips brushed mine, I let them stay for a moment, knowing that I'd never experience this sensation ever again. I didn't want to stop him but it was the right thing to do so I gently pushed us apart.

'I suppose it's a good job that we never did, you know?'

'Make love?'

'Yes. You might have ended up pregnant and that would've been a disaster.'

'I'm glad you see that now. That we could never have continued our relationship knowing we were brother and sister.'

'I do see that now. I feel like the person I loved has died. Do you?'

'Yes, I do.' I took his hand. 'But we're different people now. Siblings. And we have to learn to love each other as brother and sister rather than lovers.'

'It's not going to be easy, but I'll try.'

'We both need to. I'm going to miss you. And I don't just mean while I'm away. I mean I'm going to miss us.' I patted tears from my cheeks.

'I'll miss you too.' He hugged me again briefly before pulling himself away and starting up the car. 'I'll drop you home.'

'Thanks, Joe.' Tears filled my eyes. I wanted to scream but stayed silent.

Chapter Forty-Five

Peggy

After unlocking the front door, the cold chill hit me. 'It's freezing in here.' I charged into the sitting room, lit the gas fire and drew the heavy curtains. 'Hopefully, it'll warm up soon. I'll get some plates for the chips and put the kettle on.'

Adam kicked off his shoes, slipped into his slippers and followed me into the kitchen. 'Forget the plates. Let's eat them from the newspaper.'

'Oh yes. Let's. Somehow, they taste nicer, don't they?'

'They do.' He chuckled. 'Saves on the washing up too.'

'Do you think he's going to be okay?'

'I think he may well be. Thanks to you. You did a great job convincing Mrs Webster to speak to Rachel. Neil's been so much lighter since they cleared the air. And you, Peg, made the right decision not to go to America.'

I took the condiments from the cupboard. 'Salt and vinegar?'

'Thanks.'

'He's never going to forgive me, is he?'

'I think he might.'

'And us? Will we be okay?'

'I'm sure we will be. Come here.' Adam took me in his arms and kissed me properly on the lips for the first time in weeks.

'We could always heat these up in the oven later, you know? As we have an empty house.'

'Mr Davies, are you suggesting what I think you are?'

He grinned. 'Get up those stairs, Mrs D.'

Kate smiled showing off her slightly pink cheeks. Her face had filled out a little and lost that haggard look. I gazed at my family as we ate our evening meal. It was lovely seeing my daughter eat although I tried to avoid watching her as I didn't want her to be self-conscious. Therapy was going well and she seemed to be coping better at school.

I gathered up the plates and took them over to the sink. Adam followed me. 'I'll take Kate out for a while so you can speak to Neil.'

'But...'

'Trust me. He's ready.' Adam wandered back to the table and tickled Kate under her chin. 'How do you fancy a short stroll with your old dad?'

She glanced across at me. 'What about Mam?'

'I'll be washing up. It'll be nice for you and Dad to have a bit of a catch up.'

'Neil?' Kate asked.

Adam winked at me. 'Neil can help your mam with the dishes.'

'All right then. It'll be fun to have some Daddy time. We haven't done that for ages.'

'Wrap up warm' – I fastened an apron around my waist – 'it's Jack Frost out there.'

Adam brushed his lips against mine. 'We will, don't worry.' He whispered, 'Good luck.'

'Wash or wipe?' I smiled at Neil.

'Wash if I must.' He headed for the sink and ran the tap. As he loaded the dishes into the hot soapy water, I asked, 'How are you feeling now?'

'About what?'

'You and Rachel.' I dried the dinner plates.

'Better, but it's difficult, you know? When she was the one.'

I stroked his hair. 'I know, darling. I know. Things will get easier, I promise. And you know that your dad and I have your back.'

'I'm sorry for blaming you.' He turned to face me. 'Rachel made me see that it wasn't your fault, but I needed someone to blame.'

'I understand.' It was wonderful that he no longer blamed me but it didn't stop me blaming myself.

We carried on in silence till the dishes were done. He pulled the plug and let the water drain from the sink. 'Can we sit down and talk for a while as we're alone?'

'Of course.' I perched on one of the dining chairs and he took the seat next to me.

'This man, Rachel's father...'

'Yes?'

'Did you love him?'

'Yes, very much.'

'That's what Rachel said. So why didn't you marry him?'

'He was supposed to come back for me but never did.'

'Why didn't you keep Rachel?'

'I didn't get the chance. My father forced me to give her up. I never got a say in any of it. The nurses wouldn't even let me see her. I told your dad about her as soon as we started dating.'

'Why did your father do that?'

I blinked slowly. 'Who knows? It was something I was unable to forgive which is why I moved to London, and that's where I met your dad. When I fell pregnant with you, we couldn't have been happier but we made sure not to tell my parents until after we were married. Your dad and I always hoped Rachel would come looking for me and become part of our family.'

'Then why didn't you bring her to meet us?'

'I was wrong. I should've done. I'm sorry.'

'Yes, that was a big mistake, but like Rachel says, we can't change the past. One day I hope to learn to love her as a sister but right now, it's hard.' He held his stomach. 'It hurts in here' – he touched his chest – 'and in here. And I'm not sure how I'll ever get over it.'

'A day at a time, darling.'

'So, when you met Dad, you can't have known him long before getting pregnant. I mean there's only sixteen months difference between Rachel and me.'

'No, I didn't. You were three weeks early, mind.'

'So, did you get married because you had to?'

'No.' I stroked the side of his face. 'Not at all. We were in love.'

'But so soon afterwards?'

'I fell in love with your dad the moment I set eyes on him. Mike, Rachel's father, was in the past. He abandoned me, although he never knew about the baby. Recently, however, on meeting up with him again, I discovered my father had warned him off. Why Mike didn't persist, I've no idea. If that had been your dad, he'd never have given up. He'd have fought for me. So no, Neil, your dad and I didn't get married because we had to but because we were in love, and maybe one day' – I squeezed his fingers – 'you'll find love again.'

'Rachel said you're planning to see her off at the airport.'

'Yes. Your dad's coming with me.'

'I'm planning to ride up there with Stu. Rachel knows and she doesn't mind.'

The door slammed and Adam and Kate's voices travelled into the kitchen.

'Remember, Kate doesn't know anything yet. Once you're ready, and only then, we'll invite Rachel over. I shan't do anything until you give me the go-ahead.'

'Thanks, Mam. I think maybe Stu and I may go travelling for a while. Give me the chance to get Rachel out of my hair. You don't mind, do you?'

'No' – I hugged him – 'but make sure you have a valid reason to tell Kate so she doesn't get suspicious.'

'Don't worry, I will. And it will allow you and Dad the chance to give Kate your whole attention while she gets better.' He hugged me back.

Things were going to be all right. Adam had forgiven me, Neil still loved me, and Kate was well on the mend to a full recovery. In time we would be able to welcome Rachel into our home as a family.

Chapter Forty-Six

Rachel

Dad helped the driver unpack our suitcases from the boot and put them on a trolley. Linda hooked her arm in mine. Mrs Smith and Mum chatted as they stepped from the black cab.

'Stu said he might ride up to see us off,' Linda said. 'I hope that's okay.'

'Of course. He's your boyfriend. Only natural he'd want to see his girlfriend off when she's disappearing for a month. Just because things have gone pear-shaped for Joe and me doesn't mean that you have to suffer.' I thought about Joe and his tender loving. Why did this have to happen? It wasn't fair.

Coming back to the conversation with Linda, I said, 'Joe mentioned Stu was coming. He asked if I minded if he tagged along too. I told him it was fine. Hope they're not too tired doing the journey here and back in one day.' Dad had driven us down last night and we stayed in an airport hotel, hiring a taxi this morning.

'Stu said it's easier on a bike as he can weave in and out of traffic if necessary.'

I nudged her side. 'It'll be nice for you to see him before we get on that big bird.'

'You nervous?'

'Petrified. Reckon I'll need a drink or two in the bar before getting on there.'

She laughed. 'Me too. Look how our mams are getting on. Who'd have thought it?'

'I know. Mum and Dad have really been there for me. I didn't know how lucky I was to have them as parents until all this.'

'It was really kind of them to pay the hotel room for Mam and me.'

'Mum's idea.'

Dad pushed the trolley closer. 'You girls all right?'

'Yes, thank you.' I moved from Linda and linked my arm into his. 'You know you're the best dad in the world.'

'I would say you're the best girl but I can't ...'

'Oh?'

He smiled. 'Because I'd have to say I have the best girls in the world. Your mum and I love you and Jennifer equally. Shame she couldn't come with us today but she had that important appointment with her tutor. To be honest I think she liked the idea of the house to herself for a couple of nights once I'd agreed to her friend staying.' Dad chuckled.

Mum came up behind him. 'Check-in's that way, Charles.'

'Oh yes.' Dad led the way through the glass doors.

As we rattled in, I was gobsmacked at the huge area.

Mum said to Mrs Smith, 'Look at the girls overwhelmed by it all.'

Mrs Smith said, 'I must admit to being just as stunned. Such a wide space and all those people queueing at the desk. I've never flown myself.'

I scanned the area. It was much bigger than I'd expected. Men and women in posh suits rushed in different directions. Finally, I spotted Peggy and Adam, and waved them over.

'Mum and Peggy have already met,' I said, 'so Dad, Mrs Smith, this is Peggy and her husband, Adam.'

They each nodded hello.

'It's rather sad we're not meeting in better circumstances,' Adam said.

'Very true,' Dad answered. 'Joe, sorry Neil, is a nice lad. Is he at work today?'

'No, he and his mate are making their way up here on the motorbike to see the girls off. Rachel's fine about it.' Adam faced me. 'Aren't you?'

'Yes. I am.'

Dad frowned. 'You never mentioned it?'

Peggy kept looking around and didn't appear to know what to say. I thought how much she'd changed since our first meeting when I'd met a confident woman. What had I done to her? Maybe I should never have gone searching for her. Mum said it would end in tears and she was right. Luckily, she hadn't thrown that back in my face. I probably would have done if I'd been her.

Linda and I wandered up to the woman at the desk. She opened our passports, looked at our photos and then at us. Dad put our cases on the scale. The assistant passed our flight cards and told us which gate to go through. As we turned around Stu came running towards Linda.

'Lind. Phew. Thought I'd missed you.' He took her in his arms and snogged her.

Joe stood back a few yards. Dad moved towards him. I tapped Dad's arm. 'Don't. Like I said, I told him it was okay to come.'

'Very well, as long as you're sure?'

'I am.' I walked up to Joe. 'I'm glad you made it.'

'How could I not?'

'We need to go through the gate soon.'

'I shan't get in your way.'

I held him close. 'I'll miss you.'

'I'll miss you too. To new beginnings.' He stepped back.

I turned to Peggy. 'Look after, Joe. I mean Neil.'

'I think perhaps it's me who should get used to calling him Joe. I never knew that was his preferred name. What kind of a mam does that make me?'

'A wonderful mam. He'll need time but be there for him. Mend your family that was strong and whole before I came along and fractured everything. I'll be in touch once I get back.'

'Thanks, Rachel. I'll try.'

'Everything okay?' Dad asked.

'Yep.' I repositioned my shoulder bag. 'I'm ready for an adventure with my best friend, and I think Joe and Peggy might just be all right too.'

'When did our girl suddenly grow up?' Mum kissed my cheek.

I grinned. 'I don't know.'

Adam came over and patted the top of my arm. 'Thank you for taking the time to speak to Neil. He'll get past this and then hopefully you can get to know each other again as brother and sister.'

'I hope so,' I said. 'Look after him for me.'

'I will.' Adam kissed me on the cheek.

Peggy was behind me. 'Have a wonderful trip and I'll keep my fingers crossed that you get to see a better side of Mike.'

'Me too.' I forced a laugh when all I wanted to do was cry.

'Send us a postcard.' She embraced me. 'We'd best get over there to Ne... No, to Joe.'

'Yes.' I blinked as she and Adam headed towards the back of the airport. 'I think we should head off too,' I said to Linda who was still clinging to Stu. 'We've an adventure awaiting.' I forced a smile.

'The gate's this way.' Dad slid a five pound note into my palm. 'Get a drink for you and your friend once you go through. It'll help steady your nerves for the plane. Just the one, mind.'

'Thanks, Dad.' I hugged him before turning to Mum and holding her close too. I looked towards the exit and spotted Joe, Peggy and Adam leaving the airport. They waved. I waved back.

❦

Trembling, I glanced around the bar area as I drained the vodka and lime from my tumbler. I wished I could drink myself to oblivion, not that I'd ever done that, but it might've made me forget. Although then they'd never let me on the plane. 'Are you nervous?' I asked Linda.

'A little, but excited too. We've been planning a holiday together for ages and it probably wouldn't have happened if...'

'Yep, you're probably right. That's our gate they're calling.' I rose from the black vinyl-cushioned chair. Maybe once in the air I'd be too petrified to think about Joe.

❦

The plane roared as it bumped along the runway. Lights flickered from above and overhead bins rattled. After racing along the tarmac for what seemed an age, the plane finally lifted into the air, and then there was a rumble-thump.

I peered up at the stewardess. 'What was that?'

'It's all right, pet. Just the wheels going up. This your first flight?'

I nodded.

'You'll be fine. What with drinks, snacks, meals, etc, you'll be landing in Miami before you know it.'

'I hope so.'

'Have a read or close your eyes. You'll be able to watch a film shortly. We'll be around with headphones soon.' She patted my shoulder.

As I gazed at the cotton wool clouds through the porthole it was like watching the sea's roaring waves. My stomach churned. Maybe once I'd eaten something it would settle. The stewardess said they'd be around with snacks later.

I thought back to Joe's birthday. He was so loving, his hands so gentle, his kisses so tender. When he laid me down on the back seat of the car, I imagined being in Heaven, I so wanted to give myself to him.

My gut felt like it was being torn from me. Why oh why did things have to be this way? Would I ever find anyone else to make me feel like that again?

The plane shuddered. Startled, I jumped. 'What's happening?' A woman across the aisle reached across and touched my arm. 'It's just a bit of turbulence. It'll pass shortly.'

I turned to Linda to hold her hand but she was fast asleep. My heart hammered. Eventually the plane returned to a smooth motion. I closed my eyes and tried to relax.

A year ago, I'd no idea I was adopted, yet in the last twelve months I'd had to rediscover myself, get to know my natural parents, and now I must learn to love Joe in a different way. I pictured him as my brother. Those smiling eyes. The way he laughed. The colour of his hair. I bolted upright. Why hadn't I seen it before? He was the image of Peggy. It had been staring me in the face all these months but I'd been blind. Why hadn't Jenny picked it up? She'd met Peggy and Joe, but then I suppose she hadn't witnessed all their mannerisms. Like I'd said to Joe, we were most likely attracted to each other because of our genes. When I arrived back home we should spend time together again, learning about each other, but this time as brother and sister.

'Rach?' Linda whispered.

'Yep?'

'You okay?'

'Think so.'

'Were you having a bad dream?'

'In a way, yes. I suddenly realised how alike Joe and Peggy are.'

'I always said you and Joe had the same eyes. Not just the colour but setting.'

'You did. Perhaps I should've paid more attention.' I licked my dry lips. 'I was wondering what it would be like to have Joe as a brother.'

'That must be difficult.'

'Yes it is.'

'Do you think you'll be able to cope?'

'I don't really have a choice if I want him in my life. He can't be my husband but he can be my brother.'

'You're very brave.'

I leaned forward. 'I'm not sure about that. It's not going to be easy but with you as my best friend, Peggy, and my mum and dad, all behind me, I'll give it a bloody good try. Anyway' – I gave a chuckle – 'I've always wanted a brother.'

The hostess stopped at our seats. 'Drinks?'

'Two Asti Spumantes, please?' I grinned.

She handed me a couple of small bottles of sparkling wine and added ice to the beakers. 'Enjoy.'

'Thank you.' I poured the fizz into the plastic glasses and passed one to Linda. 'To moving forward.'

'To the future.' She clinked her glass with mine.

The bubbles warmed my stomach. This trip to Miami was just what I needed. Even Mike may prove me wrong and turn out to be a decent human being after all. 'To making new memories.' I raised my glass again.

Acknowledgements

Special thanks to my friend Maureen Cullen. Not only for her perceptive and thoughtful editing in *The Woodhaerst Triangle* but her continuous support, encouragement and faith in me.

A big thank you to my fabulous beta readers for their invaluable feedback, to my cousins, Elsa Games and Madeline Wirt, for their help around Sealand Air Base, and to Colin Ward, inasmanywords(.com), for the cover design. Credit goes to Suzi Bamblett for the phrase 'fizz'n'pips'.

Finally, a big thank you to my husband, children, family and friends for their continued support and faith in me.

About the author

Patricia M Osborne was born in Liverpool but now lives in West Sussex. She is married with grown-up children and grandchildren. In 2019 she graduated with an MA in Creative Writing. She is a published novelist, poet and short fiction writer. Her debut poetry pamphlet, *Taxus Baccata,* was nominated for the Michael Marks Pamphlet Award.

Patricia has a successful blog at Whitewingsbooks.com featuring other writers. When Patricia isn't working on her own writing, she enjoys sharing her knowledge, acting as a mentor to fellow writers.

You can find out more about Patricia by visiting her website, whitewingsbooks (.com)

Also by Patricia M Osborne

House of Grace family saga trilogy:

House of Grace (Book 1)
The Coal Miner's Son (Book 2)
The Granville Legacy (Book 3)

The Oath
A Victorian era saga

~

Poetry Published by The Hedgehog Poetry Press

The Montefiore Bride
Taxus Baccata
Sherry & Sparkly
Symbiosis
Spirit Mother: Experience the Myth
Stickleback
Nature's Bookends

Milton Keynes UK
Ingram Content Group UK Ltd.
UKHW031524290824
447545UK00005B/144

9 780995 710740